Kirsten Shonle

Psychoscribble

A Memoir on BPD and Journaling Ideas

novum pro

This book is also
available as
e-book.

www.novumpublishing.com

© 2019 novum publishing

ISBN 978-1-64268-086-7
Editing: novum publishing
Cover photo: Kirsten Shonle
Cover design, layout & typesetting:
novum publishing

www.novumpublishing.com

Table of Contents

A Note to the Reader,

Psychoscribble: Is defined as pieces of writing that help to gain clarity. It is a structured form of journaling. It is raw and comes from within. It is both creative and constructive. It can help you figure out what is truly going on in your mind especially if you like to go back and forth from reason mind to emotion mind all in a matter of seconds. It is what you want to make of it.

My psychiatrist, Dr. Daniel Price M.D., coined the term Psychoscribble. It was a joint effort to actually put Psychoscribble into action. For me, writing is where I can find my answers and look at things from all sides without judgement. In dialectical behavior therapy (DBT), the wise mind is often discussed. The wise mind is the middle ground where both your emotion mind and rational mind have equal say in the outcome. It is a place where you accept your emotions and yet look at them rationally. You are in a place where you can make wise decisions. I can reach wise mind through my writing. Everyone's recovery looks different. I am just sharing my journey and maybe it can provide ideas for you to journal about or explore on your own. If you are not planning on taking away any writing ideas from this book, I still think you can benefit from reading about the struggles and small triumphs I have gone through with my mental illness.

I have been diagnosed with Borderline Personality Disorder (BPD), Major Depressive Disorder, Generalized Anxiety Disorder, Anorexia, Alcoholism and PTSD. Throughout the book I will be touching on these parts of myself and the type of writing I did to help me gain insight. There is some overlap with what I write as everything is bound together. It's a web of my emotions and my disorders which have a lot of overlap. My major issue at this time is dealing with BPD. Some of my other issues such as suicidality and alcoholism are directly related to my BPD. This is both a memoir and a book of suggestions. I am not a trained professional. I am a person with mental illness who is working on gaining control of her life. I am still working on my journey to recovery. I am hoping writing this book will help me immensely. I am writing through my ups and downs. My psychoscribble pieces are glimpses of a BPD/addict mind. I believe that mental health providers can gain insight from my book as well.

I had started to write the psychoscribble pieces in July 2018 starting with letters to my emotions. I started to write the chapters to this book to go hand in hand with my psychoscribble the first week of October 2018; I finished the book in January 2019. The book is very raw as it takes you through my journey towards recovery. I do discuss the past in my memoir pieces. The past does affect the present. I am textbook case of BPD. I have taken bits and pieces from many forms of therapy. Writing is my favorite form of therapy.

I have been told throughout my years of therapy that journaling is a great tool to use in recovery. I have been journaling since I was twelve years old. For me, my journal looks like my monkey mind vomited on the paper. It is a stream of conscious that can lead down the path of negativity all too easily. This form of journaling can sometimes be helpful to me, but it usually isn't as I do not have direction. I am a person who doesn't like others to tell me what to do, but I found Dr. Price's writing suggestions to be very helpful. I also came up with several ideas myself. I hope you, the reader, can find your own form of psychoscribble.

I have decided to not edit any of my psychoscribble writings. I like the rawness of brain and heart to paper without judging the grammatical errors (for me it's brain to keyboard as my handwriting is worse than a chicken's). I feel that if I were to edit, then everything would be a skewed version of my thoughts and emotions. I would overthink what I wrote and would then fall down the path of perfectionism and everything would feel phony. These are basically journal ideas. Who edits their journal? I am sure there are people out there who do so. Maybe you? I try to include the dates where I can as I have grown from my first psychoscribble to the ones I am working on now.

Happy reading and journaling.

P.S.,
I swear like I get to take coins out of people's swear jars every time I do so. I wish. I'd own my own private jet to get to my own private island. So this book isn't one you would read to your kids at night. There are sexual undertones throughout the book as well. That is what works for me. You need to find what works for you.

CHAPTER ONE

My Relationship with
Borderline Personality Disorder

I diagnosed myself with Borderline Personality Disorder when I was seventeen. I had read *Girl Interrupted* by Susanna Kaysen, and she included the criterion for BPD from the *Diagnostic and Statistical Manual of Mental Disorders*, 3rd edition. I thought, oh my God, this is me to a tee. I was still young and did not have the interpersonal relationship issues (yet), but I had every other criterion. I did a little more research on the topic and finally thought I had a reason for my emotional outbursts. My brother would often say, "Kirsten is going crazy again," as I would be ripping posters off my walls. I would also tear apart a drawing or poem I had created if it was not appreciated the way I wanted it to be. My mother always said I was too sensitive. In my mind, reading about BPD made me feel like there was something wrong with me other than my depression and eating disorder.

I mentioned the idea that I might have BPD to my therapist of three years. She did not think I had the disorder. I was upset by this as I thought there was a name for the fact I would sometimes act so crazy. There was an answer to my constant need for attention and the huge fear I had about abandonment and rejection. My therapist didn't acknowledge my thoughts. I felt rejected. She was my therapist and she obviously knew better than I. I thought maybe I wanted to have BPD to help give me a sense of identity. Aside from being thin, I had no idea who I was, trying on all kinds of different personas and never finding one that fit. My therapist and I continued to just work on my eating disorder and talking about superficial bullshit.

After a suicide attempt when I was twenty, I ended up in a mental hospital. The psychiatrist at this mental hospital validated me and diagnosed me with BPD. I was like, finally. I am not just crazy in my own head; I really have a reason for my fears and screaming fits. Of course, he also invalidated me by saying that I was intelligent so I should be able to beat BPD, no problem. What the fuck does being intelligent have to do with getting better? This is a question I have fought with for over twenty years as other professionals or crisis hotlines have said this same thing to me. If being smart could make me better, then wouldn't I have used this intelligence to do so by now? It's not like I woke up one morning and was suddenly smart. However, my busy brain being the way it is, would think, well if my intelligence cannot get me better, maybe I want to remain sick and miserable? I would then get very angry at myself and cut or burn my skin as both a way to ground myself, feel something other than the empty pit, and to punish myself.

I was still seeing the same therapist I was seeing at the age of seventeen and told her that I do have BPD. A psychiatrist diagnosed me with it in the hospital. She said that I do not have BPD and the psychiatrist only saw me for a week a had jumped to the diagnoses prematurely, probably because I cut and burn myself. Again, I wasn't validated, and I just went back to talking about my eating disorder and why I got really pissed off at a driver on the road. I was so pissed I drove recklessly and ended up tailgating the driver at ninety miles per hour before I swung around him and dropped down to sixty-five miles per hour. One would think that telling a story like this would be validating of my disorder, but it wasn't.

I went years of knowing I had BPD, but I also kept telling myself that I was wrong. I told myself that I just made it all up. I read a book, and I thought it was a good personality to have because I did not know who the fuck I was. I truly thought I was mimicking the disorder like some kind of insane copycat. I am a person who needs validation from several people as I cannot self validate. I need for people to agree with my thoughts, in this case having BPD, or they are not true. This is probably one of the reasons why I have cheated on everyone I have ever been with. I need more than one person telling me I am beautiful or

I really am ugly. I need several people to tell me I am smart or I am very stupid. The list goes on and on. I have definitely put my significant others in a sewer pipe of shit. I needed another professional to tell me I had BPD to validate it, and I was not getting that support.

I had gone through a couple of therapists after my teenage/early adulthood therapist. We just talked about my daily life stressors and things along those lines. I had mostly recovered from my anorexia at this point in time. I had started dating women, and they didn't care if I was fat or thin. This was a breakthrough I had finally made on my own after years of being in and out of eating disorder clinics. I liked the two therapists I saw as people. I never mentioned the idea that I had BPD to either of them, fearing that I wouldn't be validated yet again. Both of the women ended up moving away, and I cried for days that I no longer had a friend I paid to talk to me. When the second therapist moved away, I had decided to give up on therapy as all therapists will leave me. I felt incredibly abandoned and knew rationally that they were just moving away and they weren't leaving me, but my emotions took over and made me feel as if was my fault and I should never have a therapist again because she would leave me too.

My intense emotions always led me to screaming and hurting myself. I kept trying to run away from my intense emotions. It is impossible to run away from yourself though. I found ways to ease the pain, such as working up to eighty hours in a week. I also found relief in a bottle. These were just masks hiding my pain. I was still very sick. I thought I was better as I was rarely cutting or burning myself. I figured a lot of people drink and this is a great way to numb out my emotions. I stopped believing I had BPD at this time. I mean, in my many years of treatment only one professional diagnosed me with the disorder, so he and I were obviously wrong.

I got pregnant and married when I was twenty-six years old. I was a workaholic during this time as I knew I couldn't drink. I met my husband, Jason, at work and he was married to another. I got pregnant before he was divorced. Even though he did leave his ex, Kelly, for me, I still felt like he loved her more. I would fantasize about beating Kelly up. I would have this thought multiple times a day. My jealousy took over my life. I would make up all kinds of things in my head to validate my feelings that he did not love me. He was going to leave me at any moment. Being a workaholic wasn't enough to keep me distracted. I started to have some of my eating disorder behaviors come back. When I mentioned to Jason I was becoming bulimic again, he slapped me across the face. I felt like I deserved it and this was another reason why he loved Kelly more than me.

I desperately clung to Jason even when he had physical outbursts and I would be bruised. I am not easy to live with as I regularly scream at him that he was or is going to leave me. Still to this day I question his love for me. I constantly questioned his motives and not trusting what he said to me that I was his only true love. Sometimes I would scream at him that he got physically abusive. I had a love-hate relationship with the abuse. I felt like I deserved it, and yet I also thought I was justified in throwing it back in his face. He told me the abuse was because he has never felt so much passion for anyone and he feared for the life of his child. The abuse wasn't frequent, but after five years I had enough and called the cops on him. Per the court, he had to take a year-long class to help regulate his passionate outbursts towards me. The class changed him for the better. The only other times he would lay a hand on me was when I was suicidal and he had to keep me safe.

I continued to try and run away and throw a blanket over my emotions. After my third and last child was born, my alcoholism really started to posses me. I was working at the phone company at the time. It was a good union job, and it paid better than I would have been paid even if I got my masters degree. The golden handcuffs is a term frequently used by the union workers. No one cared for the job especially with all we were put through, but the pay could not be beat. I truly believe I have PTSD from working there. I have nightmares and everything. Not only was it a sales job (not my thing), but it was a business that was managed by sheer incompetency. Our systems were a mess, and we had to disappoint customers on a daily basis. "I am sorry, the tech will not be out today, we do not know when the tech will get out there." As an empathetic person, I really felt bad for these customers as the company would continue to abuse them over and over again. A lot of my coworkers were able to become numb to the situation and could nonchalantly say, "Oh, there won't be a tech out." They would say it in a way that was so matter of fact and that since it happens all of the time the customer shouldn't be so upset.

I mostly worked as a service assistant at the phone company, as I hate sales and pushing products that people do not need. As a service assistant, I answered other representative questions or took over escalated calls. When a customer asked for a supervisor, that was me. I really had no more authority than any of the sales representatives there. I took a lot of angry customer calls. Many customers swore and called me names. I could hardly blame them; we have pushed off their installations multiple times. I would profusely apologize to the customer and agree it was not acceptable. If they apologized for swearing, I said, "I would be carrying on more than you are right now if I was in the same boat." I really wanted to help people, but if I am not given the proper tools it made it impossible to perform my job well. I felt like a failure all because of the system issues and lack of technicians. I took it to heart that I couldn't help. I couldn't do anything correctly, and I was an incompetent jerk. If I asked a manager for help with a particularly difficult situation, they would tell me to use an inefficient tool and I would be in the same place I was before. Picture needing to chop down a huge tree that is completely blocking your path. You ask for a tool to chop down the tree so you can continue on your path. Someone hands you a spoon, "Here, try this." "Ah, thanks, I guess."

I would go home every night and drink my emotional pain away. I had an empty void within me that needed to be filled. I would imagine killing myself in various ways. I would drink until I was blackout drunk and pass out. I would go into work hungover the following day. Rinse and repeat. This was my life for years. I was hardly cutting myself during this time, so I thought alcohol was a magical cure. I actually thought I was doing well. My fears of abandonment and rejection were at an all-time low as liquor made it all go away. I stopped fantasizing about killing Kelly. I still had extreme emotional outbursts when I was drunk. I attributed my screaming matches with Jason as a part of being drunk. I thought it had nothing to do with my mental health. My biggest regret while drinking was that I would sometimes yell at the kids. Even worse, when I was blackout drunk, I announced at one time that my youngest child was my favorite. What kind of parent does that? The following day I had to say that I was misinterpreted. It was hard to skirt around the issue as all three children heard what I had said. I did not remember when this happened but from the following conversation I had with my children, I know I said it. One of the things I wish I could take back, but now I just have to accept it happened. I hated being such a mess but the fact that I felt my soul was ripped out of my body, I was coping the best I could. The drinking helped with my emptiness and everything else I did not want to feel. It kept taking more and more alcohol to achieve the same results. I wanted to prove to myself that I wasn't an alcoholic by limiting myself to six pounders a night (I allowed a lot more Friday through Sunday). They were not having the same effect so I stopped eating and only drank. I dropped down to 89 pounds before I finally checked myself into rehab.

Why I finally decided to try rehab was because I was told by a psychiatrist in a mental hospital, Spring Harbor, that if I stopped drinking I would feel better. I had to admit that I did feel like my drinking was causing a lot of extra emotional turmoil. I had befriended someone online, and we had an intense emotional affair that was ripping my marriage apart. I was so caught up in drinking I did not see what was wrong about this affair. I was stuck in my own little world and was shutting out my family. I needed to do something. I tried but could not get sober on my own.

The triggering event for this hospital stay in August of 2017 was the fact that I threatened, on social media, to kill the management team at work if I had a gun. One of my union sisters brought what I wrote to management's attention. If the phone company was not a union job, I am sure I would have been instantly fired. I was not fired but put on indefinite suspension. I explained I was suicidal and an alcoholic. They told me to get help and that would shorten my time off without pay. I ended up in the emergency room that afternoon and Spring Harbor the following day. I had mentioned in the hospital that I was diagnosed with BPD when I was twenty, but I wasn't sure if I still had it. The psychiatrist put it down in my file; he did not see the diagnoses as being far fetched. The more pressing issue at the time was my alcoholism and my suicidal and homicidal ideation. This was the focus of this first visit.

In November of 2017, I ended up going to detox and then rehab. It was easy to be sober in rehab. When I got out in December, it was very difficult to remain sober. Through hard work, determination, and just being purely stubborn, I was able to talk myself out of running out for a drink every time I had a craving. I played a game with myself. Every time I did not give in and have a drink it was a win for me. AA did not work for me but I found SMART (Self Management and Recovery Training). It is a recovery program that focuses on science. There is involvement of CBT (Cognitive Behavioral Therapy) as well as REBT (Rational Emotive Behavior Therapy) in the workbook. Doing many cost-benefit analyses really helped get me through. For me, the only time I can see clearly is when I write down something and it is in black and white, clear as day.

After being sober for about 100 days, my mental illness slapped me in my face. I was back to feeling suicidal and worthless yet again. It was really hard to be at the phone company and not have an escape to run to afterwards. I ended up suppressing a lot of my rage and sadness. I was a shaken seltzer water bottle and ready to explode. I told myself that the best place to kill myself would be at work. I concocted a whole plan where I would go out to the woods and take a bunch of pills and wrap a plastic bag around my head. By the time they realized I was not coming back from my lunch break and that my car still remained in the parking lot, I would be found dead. I wrote a very brief suicide note, and I was going to leave it on my keyboard at work. Life was too hard. Killing myself at work would be poetic, showing that it is a toxic environment and management needed to make some changes before we all just die. The thought of my suicide was so clear. I knew it was a matter of time before it would actually happen.

I barely made it through the month of March. Luckily I had taken a couple three-day weekends to get me through. By April, I just could not take my pain any longer. I brought several bottles of my anxiety pills to work with me. I couldn't trust myself; I texted Jason from work and told him how suicidal I was. He called management, so they pulled me off the phones to talk to me before Jason could come and pick me up. I went straight to the ER and ended back at Spring Harbor. In my mind, it was just going to be a refresher before going back to being a tortured slave at the phone company. I mean, I was sober and I had started to practice mindfulness and meditation techniques. I felt like I should have been doing a lot better than I was. I felt a little relief at the hospital. This stay was ten days. I ended up doing a ten day partial hospital program afterwards. Partial hospital is an outpatient program with intensive classes for five hours a day. This was my second time through the partial program. I had gone the first time at the end of August. In August my brain was floating in alcohol, so I didn't gain what I could have. I thought the second time at partial was going to cure me. As on paper, I should have been doing awesome. I was sober and had a lot of coping skills already. I felt better, but that was only when I was actively in the program. As soon as I was back to work, I pictured new ways of killing myself. Again, I really wanted to do it at work because fuck those guys.

It wasn't long before I ended up back in the ER and then blue papered to go to Spring Harbor. My insurance company must have hated me. I could not stop the thoughts of suicide. My life was supposed to be better as I was sober, but my life was worse with every waking moment. This time the psychiatrist deemed that my biggest issue was having BPD and being chronically suicidal. I was white papered at the hospital and only became a voluntary patient on my court date. It did not help when I would say things like, "The hospital was a life support machine keeping me alive, and I should be able to leave so I could pull the plug and die." Sometimes I cannot help being overly dramatic even if it would hinder me in the long run. The psychiatrist at the hospital reached out to Dr. Price who specializes in BPD. Dr. Price agreed to take me on as a patient. It was only on this condition that they would let me leave the hospital as my chronic suicidality was not decreasing.

After this three week stay at Spring Harbor, I had decided I could not go back to work right away as I had done the other times. I thought that would prevent me from any further suicidal gestures. However, hating my job was not the only demon I was facing. I really needed to look at my life. Why did I so desperately want to die? It seemed like I was stuck and nothing was going to change. Things were not going well in my marriage. I was confused as to what I wanted to do. I love Jason, but I also miss dating women. I still am not sure how I can make my marriage whole again. I guess almost every marriage is a work in progress. Why should I be so special that it wasn't going to be like that for me?

There was an IOP (intensive out patient) program my social worker at Spring Harbor thought I should participate in. During this hospital stay, it was determined that I wasn't getting better because of my BPD and I had not done any form of DBT (Dialectical Behavior Taherapy) yet. I figured it would be difficult to go to work for seven hours and then do the program for three hours in the evening. This was further confirmation to delay going back to work. I felt guilty being out on short-term disability as much as I had, but I still was chronically suicidal and not getting any better. Unfortunately, I was unable to participate in the IOP because I was too suicidal. This was a rejection that hit me hard. It was going to be up to me and Dr. Price to find solutions to tone down my thoughts of death. I still took the time off from work.

Unstructured time is really hard for me. I tried to absorb everything I could about recovery from BPD.

I attended a weekly group about BPD for six weeks which started at the end of June. I already knew a lot about BPD, but it was the policy of Maine Medical Center's Outpatient Psychiatry Department that a class like this needs to be completed before I could move into a group such as DBT or Mentalizing. Dr. Price happened to run the BPD group, and he thought that for me and my textbook case of BPD, that DBT would be the best bet. As I was going to be doing DBT I needed to have a DBT therapist. This was fine by me as I fired my last therapist for perceived abandonment.

I had attempted to go back to work in July. I took an overdose of Tylenol and ibuprofen on July 3rd at work and ended up in the ER yet again. This time I was released as I had an excellent psychiatrist who stood up for me and my case. I hadn't overdosed on anything life threatening as I did not take enough Tylenol to cause irreversible liver damage. I returned to work on July 5th. This was an incredibly stressful day as a lot of my coworkers had taken the day off and we are always very busy after a holiday. The following few days at work were more and more painful. It was hard to suppress my emotions. I felt like crying all of the time. I brought a utility knife with me to work and would cut myself all throughout the day to have some sort of relief. The building was being renovated, and it was incredibly loud. My anxiety was through the roof. How can I talk on the phone with this noise? I ended up walking out on July 10th. The tenth was the last day I physically worked for the phone company. I talked to the crisis hot line on the phone and decided I had to go to the ER again to keep me safe. The job was literally killing me. I needed to find a new job as soon as possible.

I went to a crisis stabilization unit for several days but left as I was bored to tears. Dr. Price had a week off from work and that scared me shitless. I ended up doing the partial hospital program again. This was my third time doing it, and I was going to throw my all into the program. This was when the idea for *Psychoscribble* was conceived. I had taken ideas from the program and started to write letters to my emotions.

In August, I had started the DBT group. I was having a hard time grasping some of the concepts. It seemed too simplistic to actually do anything for me. I was told I needed to continue with the group even when I would express that it was not helping me much at all. I still was out on short-term disability, so I had the time and needed something to do. I always did my assignments for DBT, but it was always half-assed. I knew that DBT has helped out thousands of people with BPD. I also knew it was not the only answer, at least not for me. A few of the DBT concepts have helped me but many have not. I'm still holding out for the treatment that will be created that will be a step beyond DBT. There has to be a psychologist out there working on it now. Fingers crossed on that at least. Since the next treatment beyond DBT has yet to be developed, I needed to add something else to my treatment. I needed something unique. I had the writings that Dr. Price would assign to me to help me get beyond my borderline symptoms. I would quickly write his requests. After a little while, I couldn't just wait to have work assigned to me. I had come up with my own ideas for pieces to write. I already had a few of his suggestions under my belt, so I could create on my own work without needing to have an assignment. I feel like the only time I come close to wise-mind is when I am writing.

As I type this, it is the end of October 2018 and I still do not have a job. I am trying to use psychoscribble and a few bits and pieces from DBT to help me feel alive. I mean, if I am not going to kill myself, I want to live and not just go through the motions of being human. This is the hardest work I have ever done. I thought getting sober was the most difficult, but I was wrong. Having BPD is difficult, but it does have its good qualities too. I wouldn't be empathetic and feel love and joy as much as I do if I was only diagnosed with major depressive disorder. I do not loathe my disorder but rather embrace it. I was the one who thought she had BPD in the first place. It wasn't until now, at the age of forty-two, that many professionals agree. It is a relief to know that I am ill and the possibility of getting better is quite high.

The Guest House

This being human is a guest house.
Every morning a new arrival.
A joy, a depression, a meanness,
some momentary awareness comes
as an unexpected visitor.
Welcome and entertain them all!
Even if they're a crowd of sorrows,
who violently sweep your house
empty of its furniture,
still, treat each guest honorably.
He may be clearing you out
for some new delight.
The dark thought, the shame, the malice,
meet them at the door laughing,
and invite them in.
Be grateful for whoever comes,
because each has been sent
as a guide from beyond.
– Jelaluddin Rumi

from *Rumi: Selected Poems*, trans Coleman Barks with John Moynce,
A. J. Arberry, Reynold Nicholson (Penguin Books, 2004)

CHAPTER TWO

Letters to My Emotions

The birth of *Psychoscribble* was with my letters to my emotions. It was a new way for me to look at things. I had been able to name my emotions. I was even able to recognize the sub-emotions that would stem off from the emotion that was more prominently in my face. For me, however, just being able to name an emotion did not do anything for me. It was like, "Oh, I am feeling depressed and do not want to do anything productive. Now I am feeling sad as I have no motivation. Now I am feeling worthless as I cannot do anything." I would just fall into that loop. It happens with almost every emotion for me except for pleasure. For some reason or other the pleasure just stops there. I will feel contentment and pleasure deeply, but unfortunately they are not emotions that like to stick around for long. Wouldn't it be great if joy would spiral to more and more joy?

My third time through the partial hospital program, I needed to up the anti and do something different. If I was going to be out of work, yet again, I needed to take something new and unique out of the program. I did not want to waste my time. I needed to put work in to be able to get a return. I had never had so many suicidal thoughts and attempts as I did in 2018. In rehab, I had written a letter to my addiction and found that to be a clarifying experience. I decided to write letters to my various emotions that I was strongly feeling in July 2018. I was facing every emotion with great intensity. I wanted to ignore them, but they wouldn't shut up. Like babies, they kept screaming louder and louder at me looking for validation. Pick me up and hold me, don't put me in the dumpster.

I was exposed to the idea of The Guest House my second time in partial hospital. It is a concept adapted from thirteenth century poet, Jeleluddin Rumi (the poem is prior to this chapter). The idea is not only accepting every emotion but embracing them. We have every emotion for a reason. I had struggled with this thought of embracing emotions at first because I was like, what good is depression or apathy? As I thought about it longer, it made perfect sense. It is best to listen to the emotion rather than trying to stifle it and push it out of existence. I was always looking to run away from all of my emotions. This is why it was so easy to turn to the bottle for relief. Covering up your emotions just eventually makes things worse. Just as it is impossible to run away from yourself, it is impossible to run away or hide long from your emotions. They will catch up to you in one way or another.

I wrote my letters trying to embrace the emotions. This was something I had never done before. In my monkey-mind journaling, I would often just yell at my emotion to go away. I acknowledge that there is validity in telling your emotion what you don't like about it. Even if you are telling depression that you never want to see him again and how he has ruined your life for so many years, there is much to gain. You are acknowledging the emotion and putting words to it. You aren't trying to push the emotion away; you are facing it. For me, I like to personify my thoughts and emotions. It helps me connect better and yet stay objective. If it is easier for you to write to the emotion just as it is and you can only think of negative things to say, go for it. At least you are accepting the emotion and not trying to push it away. For many, this is a great first step to take.

My social worker at the partial hospital program (July 2018) really enjoyed the letters I was writing. I was at my wits end regarding my job at the phone company. I told him that the job seemed to rip the soul right out of me. He suggested I write to my "Souless Self." This was the most difficult piece for me to write. I was trying to stick with the same theme where I embrace each of my feelings for the positives that they have in my life. I had a huge struggle trying to figure out why feeling like I had no soul was not necessarily a bad thing. I mean how can you love yourself if you feel like you are without a soul? This writing took me over an hour. I was crying almost the whole time I was writing it. I know it would have been easier to just focus on the negatives that the feeling produces within. As I wrote and wrote and cried and cried, I eventually came up with the reason why that feeling existed and its intention. It is not the best of my writing. Overall, I am glad I wrote the piece as I was able to step back and look at what I was doing to myself by continuing to work for the phone company. The job pays very well, but money is not everything. I knew then that I needed to find a new job once my short-term disability expired.

My emotions are personified in my examples, duh. There are a lot of sexual undertones; no, why lie, there is a lot of sexual imagery in my letters. Don't worry, it is not too graphic. I did say this was not a children's book, remember? My emotions seem like they have been trying to seduce me. I take this raw feeling and gain access to more understanding. Again, this is what works for me. Everyone has their own unique style of writing and for relating to their emotions. I would encourage you to address your emotions in the way you see fit. Heck, reach out to your emotions through art or music. Whatever genre works best for you. The point is to acknowledge your feelings. Listening to them rather than trying to push them away can be helpful in your recovery. I find it helpful in mine. It also doesn't hurt to write to pleasant emotions as well. I wrote one letter to contentment. So far in my journey, this was the only pleasant emotion I have felt. Not every letter is specifically to an emotion, but my emotion mind rules everything I wrote about here. I wrote these letters in July 2018. Most of them only took twenty to thirty minutes to write, so it is not a huge time commitment.

Dear Depression,

I am always reminded of Eeyore when I look at you. Of course you are a grown man and not a cartoon donkey. I think it's how you hang your head down as you are sitting on my couch. I do not know how you could stay in that position all day long. I feel pain in my neck and back just looking at you. You don't feel the pain?

You have always been on my couch, for as long as I can remember. Sometimes you have been lying down and are out of site. I know your presence is always near. I can just feel that sadness which is always accompanied by emptiness. You have been known to engulf me. You ask me to sit on the couch next to you and the next thing I know is your heavy, gray blanket is pinning the both of us down. I have that feeling of being super empty and sad and yet feeling weighed down at the same time. I hate not having the motivation to try and get up. I become stuck with you in an endless loop inside my mind.

I know everyone gets sad on occasion and it is an important emotion to have. Why is this weighted, helpless, empty, sadness a part of my life? As I said before, you have always been around, you are just more fierce sometimes over other times. So, I'm sure like all of the others you have been a part of my life for some reason. I know between yourself and Anxiety, I have become a master at isolating. I know I started to isolate years ago so I could just sit in my own head and live in a fantasy world I have created. I truly do not know why I needed to live in an alternate reality. It was something I did from the age of eight going forward. I cannot remember anything happening to me that would cause this need to break away into my own world. I do know you helped lead the way there. So, maybe I just started having depression when I was eight and you helped me find a way to deal with it.

As an adult I still isolate for several hours during the day, but I do not try to see myself in a different world. So what are you giving me as an adult? Is it that you are giving me a reality check that life is going to be hard? Is it something I need to work at? Are you giving me permission to cry? Yes, I never wanted to cry when I was younger as I did not want to risk being called a baby. I still do not see why you are still with me. Even the pills that are supposed to make you subdued haven't put a dent in you. I must ask, what do you want from me? I also need to ask, what are you doing for me?

Ok, I appreciate you speaking to me, you are helping me work with my anger. As a kid, I had so many physical angry outbursts. You are with me so I turn that anger inward. This is why you are so strong. I need to ask of you. Please stop taking almost all of my anger to turn it inward. Yes, you have prevented me from swearing at a customer or a manager at work. You have helped me to not yell at the children (that would have been misdirected anger anyway). You have prevented me from getting physically violent in many of a circumstance. I just can't keep feeding you.

Oh? That's what you want from me. You want me to stop suppressing so much of my anger. You are getting tired after these 34 years. What had originally been the best plan for the circumstance, is no longer working. Ok, we need to come to a truce. I will do my best to deal with anger in a healthy way. You need to try your best to let me out from under the blanket. Deal? Deal.

Sincerely,
Your Easily Angered Host

Dear Anger,

You always appear so quickly. It's like you come out of the woodworks. You arrive hot and heavy. Your breathing is shallow and the sweat pours off your forehead. This is when you come knocking at my door. I do have to apologize for the fact that I jump and let out a gasp when you do arrive. I just expect that you would have been courteous and gave me a call before arriving. Even calling two minutes in advance would be a nice warning. I know, I know… You keep telling me that you do not own a phone. I am calling bullshit. Everyone has a cell phone nowadays. My friend, Negativity, most certainly has a cell phone. If you cannot get one, then find another way to warn me such as a soft knock on the door, and gradually knock louder until I let you in. You are turning bright red and the sweat droplets are pooling under your arms. Is my accusation going to cause you to flip over my chairs and smash my TV? Ok, fine. I say do it. Material items can always be replaced. I am sure you are seething right now. I can see it in your eyes. You are furious that I am telling you that you can do as you please. You like, no, *need*, the opposition. It's what feeds you. I can still feed you as you are welcome here in my head, but I am going to be feeding you fruits and vegetables instead of gummy bears and chocolate. Wow, so a hissy fit is what you are throwing right now? Ok, that's fine. I don't mind watching you try to turn over my dining room table. It's heavy, right? So you are going for the TV. Oh, no, wait, you are going for the PS4. That's fine, as long as you respect me, my dendrites and my body, you can do as you wish. I am going to ask you, however, to come and take a power hike with me. I might even scream and listen to your favorite music really loudly. Come on, it'll be fun. We might even become friends. No? Too much kindness again? Frankly, Anger, I don't give a shit. You are in my head and you will need to respect my head and what I want to do.

Sincerely,
Your Host

Dear Anxiety,

I am aware that you knocked rapidly at my door. You just needed to get in and I understand that. I do apologize that it took me longer than a minute to let you in. I am sorry that you were worried that I wouldn't answer the door. You probably feared that I was dead. I have a lot of people come and stay with me in my cozy room in-between the dendrites. So I do not know who will be at my door at any given moment. Plus, I might be comforting someone else, like our friend, Depression.

Oh, I think I probably just said the wrong thing. Just because I comfort others does not mean I do not care about you. I would give you a spare key but sometimes I need to focus on a particular moment in time. I cannot let you take me over. Yes, you do serve a purpose. If I was not concerned about what the future holds, then I would be letting Apathy take over. You keep me concerned about the future. You do not tell me the future is going to just be unicorns farting out rainbows. You tell me to be cautious. Sometimes I get a little too cautious. There are certain risks I regret not taking. You were probably right though. I might have failed miserably and then Depression and Negativity would be in my head, feeding off one another. I have to think though, any risk that I do take and fail at is a learning experience.

I could just picture you now as you read this letter. You are rapidly pacing back and forth and chewing on your nails. I can almost hear you say, "No, no, no, no, no." This is your kindness showing through. You care about me and the space I provide to you. You do not want me to get hurt. Well, Anxiety, pain is a part of life. I have grown to expect it. I loathe pain, but it is what it is.

So, I appreciate you being around. You have been helping me for years so I don't just randomly jump into an unfamiliar situation. You put a much needed space between me and the future. At least I have time to speculate about everything that can go wrong.

Again, sorry I haven't given you a spare key. I just cannot spend all of my waking hours thinking about things I really do not have any control over. The next time you come knocking, I will try my best to rush to the door. I do recognize your knock, it is very rapid and not too loud. So, I admit it, I knew it was you, but I was busy chatting with Depression. I care about you and need you. I just cannot take you every waking moment of the day. Please come back to me on an as needed basis.

Yours truly,
Your Host

Dear Apathy,

You definitely took me by surprise the other day. I remember gasping and grabbing at my chest when I walked into my living room and there you were, laying on the couch. There was popcorn all on the floor and our favorite comedy, Dodge Ball on the television. At least it seems to be a movie you do not hate. I realized you were just throwing popcorn at the TV. I couldn't gage your reaction to my entering the room. You always have resting bitch face or eye rolling going on. Those are your only two expressions. I would imagine you were annoyed at me. I often annoy you. I cannot help it.

I am sorry that I had to ask you as to why you were pegging *my* popcorn at *my* TV. You just rolled your eyes and shrugged. I couldn't get you to say anything. I am hoping that you will read this letter and respond. Oh, shit. I am sorry, I used the word hope. I get it, Hope is a fucking cunt. I know she has screwed me and fucked me over so many god damn fucking times. I envy you. You couldn't care less about Hope. Even if the desire seems to be a tangible desire and Hope would be gently making love to you, you seem to be able to block her out. Teach me. Teach me how. I am so tired of falling for Hope's enchantments. I know what you are going to say now, you are going to say you do not give a fuck about me and you won't teach me shit. Well, you have come into my psyche and settled in the dwelling that only exists because I killed millions of my brain cells. I wish you were replacing the space with intellect.

I am sorry, I am being mean again. I just need you to know that you are taking over too much of this empty spot in my mind. When you do not care about anything, I have a hard time caring about anything. I just find that you influence me to be a mindless robot.

So, truth be told, I do not see you going anywhere soon. You do not have anything better to do than lounge on my couch and diss my favorite comedy. We need to cohabitate this empty space in my mind. You have come back to me for a reason. I can only think that you are here so I will not be feeling too defeated going on strike again. I also think you are here to snap me into reality. I know you are an extremist, completely a black thinker, as nothing at all matters. However, you at least, do not let me believe that some deep breathing and walking is going to help with my suicidality. You do not believe coping skills will work. From my experience they work while I am using them but my desire to die comes right back afterwards. So, I guess I need to thank you for coming back. You were a huge part of my life in my early teen years. You got me through then too. So I do need to apologize for being a complete bitch when I got frustrated at you for using *my* couch and throwing *my* popcorn at *my* television at *my* favorite comedy.

So as I am letting you stay here, would you please stop encouraging me to cut myself where the scars are noticeable to everyone. I do not want to be wearing long sleeves all the time. If this is too much as I need to cut, and you do not care for the consequences, so more likely than not they are going to be prominent. Whatever, my scars will tell a story of the pain I am in and I have survived.

Sorry,
Your Somewhat Caring Host

Dear Boredom,

I am going to say good morning, but I wish you wouldn't take over my room. You are like a storm cloud stretching out. Like the elephant, don't talk about the huge cloud in the room. The cloud might turn black, causing an emptiness, a pit of despair. When you turn black, there is no getting around you. I used to love spending time with myself in my head, now my mind is stagnant, it doesn't change. Everything is exactly the same. I speak out into the hollow space, when you are around the echoes are muffled. I cannot do anything but sit and stare out into space. One would think that you would make meditating easier as there is not much going on between my ears here. But, no, for some reason meditating is more difficult. Maybe it's because I cannot rely on the echoes to take my mantra or focus word to a different level.

I am still trying to figure out why you have been camping out here for so long. It's been since February, right? I can almost hear you whisper no… So, what, you have been here longer then? Oh, you have been here most of my life? You are just able to take up more space when I am not feeding my addictions. Well, touché, so why are you here? I wish you could answer me right at this moment, so I guess I need to figure it out myself. They say everything happens for a reason, so every emotion happens for a reason as well. You have been around most of my life, I have to go back to when I was a kid to figure this one out.

Oh, snap. I remember now. You are the reason why I liked to spend time in my head. You are the reason why I would play board games by myself. You are the reason why I got into art and writing in the first place. You are taking over my room so I have to fend for myself, well shit. You are back in full force, now that I am sober and am not drowning millions of brain cells. I was never thinking clearly when I was an alcoholic. So you were muffled when my brain cells died. You are here now so I can give birth to new brain cells. You are here so I can look inward for self satisfaction rather than searching for it through outside forces.

I am so sorry. I don't know why I thought you were here to be mean and make my life miserable. I was so wrong. Thank you. I appreciate your stubbornness in taking over my room. I need to feed you. I need to feed you with stories and music and art. This is all you have been seeking. You have been seeking it for years. I starved you for years. You are looking out for me. I have been a horrible host. I promise I will take care of you. Please continue to take up as much space as you want. I obviously need boredom in my life. I hope you will forgive me.

Selfishly,
Your Host

Dear Suicidal Ideation,

Oh, how I adore you. You have wrapped your arms around me so many times, from the age of fourteen going forward. You were one of my first loves. Your pale skin and almost white hair is enchanting. Your stone-cold, blue eyes look right into my soul. You have very slight curves that can be seen under your white dress. My breath is taken away every time I look at you. You always blow me a soft kiss that becomes a butterfly that lands on my cheek. Your meek, soft, seductive voice gently tells me what to do.

Today, I have been told, that the end game of our plan cannot be fulfilled. The word indefinite was used, so maybe we can complete our hard work together in a week, but it might not be for over a year. Yes, I reluctantly agreed to this proposition. I am sorry. Trust me, I feel like someone has pierced my heart. This being said, I am going to have to ask you to leave. We should be on a break.

No, I am not breaking up with you. I said a break, not a break up. I cannot fully break up with you because I do still need you at times. I have a hard time letting go. Oh, come on. I am not being a tease. You are the one who has been a tease for so many years. You flirted with me back when I was in eighth grade. You told me that if I just cut my wrists I could make all of the girls shut up. Then you performed your classic blowing of a kiss and you showed me how to cut my wrists. The blood dripping off of your arms, was so bright against your pale cold body. It was like blood on snow. I really wanted to mimic you but I was not as brave. I chose a razor and did not cut deeply enough. You did not laugh at me. It was the effort that counted. You told me to take pills instead. Again, I only took 15 Sudafed. You never called me a fool. You just kissed me on my cheek and said I would succeed at some point, when all else fails. This was how it continued on for years.

You have been so close to me this last year. Our relationship has gone from being teenage friends to adult lovers. You tell me ways to off myself just after I make you cum. I have flirted with several of these methods and thought the time was coming where it would only be the two of us for the last moments of my life. I imagined it would have been very beautiful. We would be wrapped in each others arms, becoming one entity.

I ran into several issues lately. My perfect combo of pills is gone. During my visit to the emergency department in early July I was told I had to give up the pills so I could avoid being blue papered. They told Jason about them and I had to give him my bag before he ripped my room apart. I am so saddened about this, what am I to do now? I have to go with risky pills instead of my perfect cocktail. The over the counter pills are risky as they can have lasting effects on my body if they do not succeed in killing me.

I am going to miss you guiding me to different websites to do the research on how to die. You are my muse, Always, your arms are wrapped around me. Your soft lips are kissing my neck. I am going to miss you so much.

You ask why am I leaving you as I am so clearly madly in love with you still? You say I can still have you in my life, I just cannot act on the thoughts. I know. But it is so hard. I love fucking you, I really do. But it brings me too close to the act. I want to scream out, as the thought excites me so. I have been fucking you multiple times a day and look where it has gotten me? I've been in the Emergency Department and Spring Harbor so many times in this last year. You always give me the ideas or so beautifully show the example of the results with your body. You are the perfect model. This is all done after we are making love. There is definitely a correlation that after our closeness I end up acting out your ideas. We used to just flirt heavily with one another for years. Over this last year we are like a couple of young rabbits. I have noticed the difference in my actions. I was not gathering items in preparation to kill myself until we started fucking on a regular basis. I wasn't waking up every morning imagining my last moments. I wasn't thinking about my plan to die step by step at least 100 times a day. So, yeah, you have affected me. I have to say goodbye for now.

I know you have served me well in the past. I got a comfort knowing someone would show the way. I guess the lesson here is to not mix sex with business. Our professional relationship was a lot better. It would give me something to think about to get out of my painful moment in time. So yeah, we need to take a break. We need to be partners again. If I am constantly thinking about you, I am going to break my promise. So, goodbye, for now. I am truly grieving for this loss.

Love,
Your Partner

Dear Frustration,

Wow. Today was crazy. I understand why you were here. I do not know how you broke down my door and like a whirlwind you trashed everything in sight. Well, you certainly got my attention. You held my attention for almost a full hour.

I do not even know how to describe your unique energy. If Anger and Anxiety had a baby and then that baby idolized Negativity, that's who you are. I was so overwhelmed with your intensity. Shit, I am still shaking a little right now and that is after the mile long power walk. Oh yeah, and what was up with you bitching, bitching, bitching to me as I was walking. I couldn't listen to the music my air pods were providing me. I was too distracted to try and incorporate a five senses grounding portion to my walk.

What purpose did you provide me today? Yes, I get I was going into the simple task of registering my son for soccer with a chip on my shoulder. This was the first year I did not get an email reminder about it and I kind spaced it but remembered to be guaranteed and spot it had to be done before the end of July. You arrived just after I saw that today was the last day to register. Your intensity grew and grew as I ran into road block after road block. Then we learned that the final result was that multiple credit cards and my debit card were charged about 25 plus times, so this will be something new to deal with and you are going to be by my side as I dispute thousands of dollars in charges because the Goddamn website kept erroring out. I am supposed to get a Goddamn email and a fucking confirmation number. Yeah, that never happened. Why would I think they were taking my money?

As I know you will be with me regarding this issue, and daddy Anger will probably be encouraging you adding fuel to the fire, what can I expect? I guess I have to figure out what happened today. I was doing what should have been a simple task. The multiple road blocks threw me for a loop. You were right by my side. You did tell me multiple times that what was happening was not my fault. You actually kept telling me that I was doing my best given the roadblocks. You were actually telling me very positive things. When I went for my walk I think my mind was clouded. I had on blinders. You would repeat the events that happened. Negativity actually took over. That is why my power walk did not clear my head as quickly as it should have. I needed to focus on you and then I probably would have accepted what happened and there is not anything I can do about it right now. So yeah, please be by my side when I figure out who to call to dispute the likelihood of thousands of dollars in charges. At least it was only 160.00 on my debit card. So thank you for helping me see one silver lining.

Sincerely,
Your Humbled Host

Dear Negativity,

Hey, how are you? I had no idea that Suicidal Ideation was your sister until I wrote her a letter the other day. She responded back that if I was going to stop fucking her for a bit, I should stop fucking her sister, you. So you two have been talking about me I guess. It doesn't bother you to be fucking the same person as your sister? I am not even going to try and figure that one out. She probably told you I have a more passionate love affair with her. It is what it is. You have been in my life for longer. I would say you came around when I was four? Not as my lover, of course, you were like my own personal bully. So it was probably at the age of four when I was in day care. I am technically closer to you over your sister.

Suicidal Ideation did remind me that I haven't written to you. I know I have mentioned you before in some of my writings, but I did not directly write to you I only wrote about you. I still cannot get over how you strangle Positivity so quickly. She might tell me that I look nice in the morning. The next thing I know you are choking her out and I think that I do not look nice, I look fat. She will say that I accomplished reading several self help chapters. You tell me it was a lazy act and I should be at work instead. If I wasn't so goddamn fucking weak, I would be on the front line and taking all of the irate customer calls.

You don't stop there. Once you whisper one thought to me there are hundreds of statements that follow. I cannot believe that other people haven't stoned me to death by now. I am the worst piece of shit on this planet. I am the fattest, the ugliest, the stupidest, most boring person on the planet. So, this is why I hooked up with your sister Suicidal Ideation. She gives me hope that there is a way out from under your grip. Of course the two of you planned it all along that I would be tossed back and forth like a ping pong ball. You get me so depressed, sad and hopeless and then you send me to her arms.

You both want me to be dead. I guess I like that. I need a plan B. Especially as my life is just getting worse. But, I made a promise. I am supposed to take suicide off the table. Yes, this is the reason why I told your sister we need a break. I would say the two of us need to take a break as well. I know that isn't going to happen.

No, it is not just because I need someone to fuck. Well, it is nice to have someone to try and make me cum. I always enjoy going down on you at least. I digress, I know you will be around as, frankly, I need you. You keep me from being in a fantasy world. You put a realistic spin on everything. As I know I am not some hot shit (as I am a piece of shit), I am not going to try to do something crazy like try and get a book published. You have been helpful to me in this way. You keep me under your thumb. I accept this. It would be nice if you were able to just say one thing to me at a time and not upwards of a hundred things. You will do as you will. I get it.

As You Wish,
Your Inadequate Host

Dear Soulless Self,

You are an empty shell who's filled with the spit and venom of everyone you interacted with today. You are as heavy as a boulder. That's a lot of spit and venom to carry around. I do not understand why you keep torturing yourself so much. Yes, you are a self loathing masochist. But this is low, this is really low. The heaviness keeps me in my place. Yes, that's right you are affecting me so much. You make me want to die. No, you make me know the only way out of this torture is through death. And I understand you cannot leave me. I know you are going to stay. You haven't been around since July 10, but that's because I haven't been at work. You came back today because of the thought of going back to work. This is how powerful you are.

I tried to run away from you. Beside the obvious of taking a bunch of pills and drinking a fifth of vodka and then putting a bag over my head, I called crisis. I ended up in the ER overnight and the only way I was released was to give away my suicide bag with the perfect combination of pills. So now I only have Benadryl. It is going to hurt us more than original plan. And some people will survive taking 200 pills and end up brain damaged instead. Does that sound fun to you? I definitely do not want to be brain dead. I would be too stupid to work at all and too stupid to know how to end it all. I would be able to get rid of you, lucky bastard, you would die. Oh you, fucktard. You probably want to die yourself. I just can't even deal with that thought right now. I have my own dilemma.

I cannot get rid of you because I am the primary wage earner. I cannot use Benadryl. I cannot be brain dead. I have looked for other jobs and I cannot find anything that pays more than 30,000. This makes me feel so stupid. So I am going to be stuck at a place where I am forced to lie. They call it softening the blow. Then there's my sales grubby coworkers. They don't seem to fucking care being soulless. Perhaps it is because there are a few reps like myself that will fix the issue such as the customer has internet and no need for internet or a phone with no need for a phone.

So I take the call remove product and adjust billing. Flames are forming on the side of my face. I cannot think about my coworkers without Anger bursting through my door. He is pounding his fists on my table. If I could stomach talking to these reps for more than a "Hi" in the hallway, I could ask them how they deal with being soulless. You know I cannot deal with it personally.

You are the reason why I became an alcoholic in the first place. We are supposed to accept every part of our self. I keep writing to see if something comes to me. I guess this is the first time I have had to deal with a massive flooding of tears as I do personal exploration with different aspects of myself.

You are one of the newer entities. You have only been with me for ten years. Goddamn, I wish I could have handled being the stay at home parent while Jason worked. But I couldn't, so I worked and brought home at least 90 percent of the household income. I now feel resentment peeking her head in my window. I can smile and blow a kiss to resentment, but I have not figured out how we could be friends yet. You make me feel so awful. I do not like being filled with spit and venom. I do not like feeling like my chest has completely caved in because of boulder being set upon it.

Perhaps there is a way I could make you feel more comfortable? Death? I touched upon that up above. I made a promise to my psychiatrist I won't. So I guess there isn't anything that could make you feel better while you stay here. I have to pin point what purpose do you serve?

I know being soulless is perfect for a sales representative. But I was never a sales representative. Remember the first manager I had made fun of me about my sales. I should have had a grievance written against her but I was new to the union concept back then. So I know you did not join me and all of the other characters/emotions who live in my head, in order for me to become a sales rep. I am still not a sales rep after all of these years.

I know each lie I have had to tell customers has killed a little bit of the me (I used to like) everyday. Then you appeared. I couldn't do anything when I got home except drink. I had to drink away my day. Now that I am sober I have not found the thing to calm you down and I guess since you are looking for death, I haven't been successful because I have reached out for help. Soulless, soulless, soulless. To have no soul feels like I am a useless parasite who just sucks the life out of everyone I encounter. Is the life I am sucking out of them doing anything for me? Nope. I am just destroying them. And, shit, you have a lot to do with this.

What's your take on this thought? At first you came to join me to put distance between myself and the customer. You knew I hatted the job since my first call. The money and the known increase of money, locked me into the golden handcuffs. So if I didn't really have a soul, the lying, in theory, would have been less of a blow. Unfortunately, I am actually a nice person. I worked with a teenager on the autism spectrum before working at the phone company. I liked the job. I am someone who needs to do something that I think is helpful to people. I have moral standards which makes a sales job the worst possible job I could have picked.

So you were supposed to be my buffer. However, you saw that you were not working in the way you were intended to work as I still couldn't help taking to heart every person I had to "bend the truth to". You probably liked it when I drowned out the spit and venom with 8 beers a night. Again, now that I am sober I can feel you very prominently. You are upset that you did not do your job properly. You were my drinking buddy, weren't you? You feel just as badly as I do. So now you are the one I will be going into a suicide pact with. You hate yourself just as much as I hate you. You hate yourself just as much as I hate myself. This is all because of goddamn money. I don't think we are selfish and money grubbing assholes. We are just looking to live. We still have the runaway living with us. As I said before, I am a nice person. You have good intentions but failed me because Fairpoint and now Consolidated are one of the worst places to work. It's especially hard place to work if you cannot leave the job at the work place like me. I hate that what I am forced to say to customer is coming out of my mouth. I end up owning the lie I was forced to tell. I bring each lie home with me. When you cannot have any respect for yourself because of what you have to do at work, you end up just loathing yourself. No one like parasites.

So there is just something about my personality that cannot detach myself from the job. Sorry you failed. I am going to have to ask you to leave. I know you will for the rest of the evening. I know you will return if I have to go back to that hell hole.

Tearfully Yours,
Your Sad Host

Dear Contentment,

Hey! Where the fuck have you been? I thought you had died. No, but seriously, why did you abandon me for so long? Were the others giving you a hard time? I am guessing that is the case. You had appeared every now and then over the last several years, but only for fleeting moments. Today you were with me for the whole afternoon and into the evening. I am noticing that you might be backing away right now as I am back to my old habit of sitting on my bed and closing myself off to the world.

So you are probably going to leave again soon aren't you? What? I think I can hear you in the distance. No. I do not think it is all up to me for you to show yourself and give me some relief. Ok, fine. I did keep myself very busy today. I know that really helped. Also I did drive to Auburn to visit Jaymie. It was nice chatting with her again. I definitely prefer talking with people in person. I did have a nice time even though we really didn't have anything to do. It is so nice to talk to someone who can understand my extreme outbursts. She would have reacted the same way I did to that driver from Florida. She is so much younger than I am but we get along. I am sure if we were roommates ever we would be getting into screaming fights. Like me she is text book Borderline.

So that took up my whole afternoon. When I got home, Jason was moving things in the basement so he forgot about Io's appointment. When I talked to Io asking why he did not remind Jason to bring him. He said Papa was busy. I was able to call him on why he didn't go to therapy. He just didn't want to go. So this wasn't an entirely pleasant experience I did get Io to tell me the truth. That felt good as I usually get shrugs and grunts from him. Maybe it was my calm demeanor that got him to admit the true why.

Soon afterwards, I convinced myself to go to SMART as I heard the meetings on Tuesday have been small. The meeting was very small and instead of doing the tool workshop we just sat around and chatted. One woman there went into her stressful living situation with her wife. From her description of everything I asked her if her wife has BPD. She said no, a lot of other diagnoses though. As she continued on, I was like yeah your wife very likely has BPD. So I was able to give some good advice. Well, she thought it was good advice. This made me feel really good. We chatted for like 15 minutes after the meeting. That was nice. I maybe should see about actually becoming a friend with her. They say it is best to have 5 people to reach out to. I think this is good advice.

This weekend I couldn't reach Jaymie or Jesse and so it was warm line and crises instead. I'm telling you this because you were no where to be found, even during my Key and Peele marathon. Err. So yes I feel a bit of anger creeping in. I know you will be leaving soon. Especially as I got the idea in my head that I should say fuck it to making any money and work for the intentional warm line. They are only hiring per diem right now. What the fuck is up with that? There were several times I have called and there are long wait times. They absolutely need more people manning the phones. I am trying to brush off the negative thoughts that were provoked that lead to difficult emotions. However, I am having a difficult time with this. You were with me a lot of the day and I appreciate that. I just don't want you to be such a stranger anymore. I know you cannot be around every day, and especially for not as many hours as today. Maybe you can try a couple times a week? Yes, I will try and do my part. Thanks for the pleasant visit. I hopefully will see you later this week.

Sincerely,
Your Host

CHAPTER THREE

Self-Guided Meditation

Guided meditation works for millions of people. I just happen to be one of the people it doesn't work for. I'm like, "You can't tell me what to do. I am still holding my breath in from the last time, I can't inhale again. Your voice irritates me." For these reasons I had to find my own way to meditate. I wrote a self-guided meditation in December 2017. This was a great starting point for me on meditating. I now also enjoy just listening to thunder showers and picturing things I find grounding. I like to mix it up a bit as I grow bored quickly.

If you happen to be one of the millions of people who enjoys guided meditation, then by all means skip this very short chapter. There are a lot of free guided meditations out there on the internet. Enjoy your journey finding the guided meditations that you love. If you are continuing to read this, you are at least curious about the idea of creating your own meditation. I will explain how to create a self-guided meditation.

The first step is to pick a place that you find relaxing or soothing. This could be a favorite childhood spot or a place you only went to once but it made your soul feel good. I would take a moment and just imagine the area in your mind. Are you able to see the colors and hear the sounds at this place? If you cannot quite imagine every detail about the place, you either need to keep focusing on the spot until you can fully be there, or you need to pick out a different place. It needs to be somewhere that you can travel to in your mind. A location you can teleport to and not have to take a tedious drive around your dendrites to travel to.

It is best if you can incorporate all five of your senses. What do you see? How do things feel? Listen for the sounds. What does the air smell like? Is there anything you can taste? The first three are definitely the easiest of the senses to recreate in your mind. Most people think in images and sounds and it is not a far stretch to incorporate touch. Smells and tastes can be more difficult as we don't tend to think in these senses. Perhaps your favorite place is a bakery or in a relative's kitchen. If that is the case, you have tons of smells and tastes you can incorporate into your writing. You do not need to be in a bakery, a flower garden or on a salty beach to find smells or even a taste. If you truly transported yourself to the peaceful location, I'm sure you can find that all five of your senses are engaged.

Now that you are fully at your place, you can start to write it down. Include as many details as you can remember. Is the location warm or is it cold? Do you sense that your breaths are calm at this location? Incorporate everything into your piece. Write as if you are there and not just imagining the location. What is it that makes you feel peaceful? You have to become one with your place. Once you are there, you will write something that is raw and has a lot of meaning to you.

I am sure you are thinking, "Who does this writer think she is? Reading and meditating are not the same thing. What is the point of this?" I thought you might question that. Once you write about your special location, you have created the skeletal structure. You have already imagined being there and now you have put it down on paper. Once it is written down, it helps seal the feelings you have. You not only pictured the location, you became one with it. When you go to practice your meditation just remember the basics. It is not like the meditation police are going to come and throw you into the cave of chaos. I personally have never meditated with my piece word for word. It is actually fun as sometimes things get a little more elaborate during my meditation. My deep breathing is natural. I can actually feel the warmth of the sun. I love to travel to my place when my anxiety is kicking my butt. Sometimes just picturing it is enough to take my anxiety down a notch. I hope you find this to be a relaxing writing assignment.

My Meditation

Leaves crinkle under your feet as your are climbing the peak. Pine and aspen trees create a canopy over you. You pause for a moment and take a deep breath in and just listen. So high in elevation you can only hear a few birds in the distance and the sound of the leaves in the wind. You take a moment to absorb your surroundings. You notice a tree in which a portion of the dark brown bark is missing. The bareness of the tree is auburn in shade. The urge is to walk to the tree. You want to feel the tree and its different textures. You close your eyes. The bark is rough and your fingers fall in and out of the dimples. Each different crevice feels different to your fingers. You just take a moment to notice that some areas are very rough and others aren't. Some places feel cold and some feel warm. You softly open your eyes so you can find the smooth auburn part of the tree so you can caress that. There is a stickiness to this area. You place your palm on the tree. It is slightly difficult to move your whole hand over this area. It keeps getting stuck and unstuck in the hidden glue. You decide to smell the tree. You take in a deep breath through your nose. The bark smells like butterscotch. You exhale through your mouth. You sniff in another deep breath, holding onto the aroma. You feel content in the moment, smelling the butterscotch and just listening to the leaves rustle over head.

You slowly let go of the tree and head back to the path. Your body enjoys this brief rest before continuing up the final steep incline. This is it; the moment of truth. Only five hundred more feet to go. The two-thousand-foot climb is well worth the effort. The view will be incredible. You count each step as you climb. You notice the strength of your muscles and how hard they are working to help you reach your goal.

The three hundred and sixty degree view is breathtaking. You are nine thousand feet above sea level. There isn't anybody in sight. You are alone and on top of the world. You close your eyes and take in another deep breath. You hold the breath for ten counts and slowly exhale for twelve counts. You open your eyes. The sky is a light shade of blue with a few puffy white clouds hovering. The sky is a great contrast to the surrounding mountains. Although it is July, some of the peaks have a bright white snow on them. You stare at the mountain feeling amazed at how warm you feel under the sun. How could there be snow when the sun wraps around you? You smile and feel content. You are at peace with the moment. You take in a deep breath and release the air through your mouth. Thousands of miles above any traffic, the air is crisp and fresh. The heat is causing a small droplet of sweat on your forehead. You open up your water bottle and gulp at the refreshing drink. It tastes like the best water you have ever had. As you swallow you change your position to look at green mountain that is in closer proximity. The mountain is covered in pine trees.

You notice the sun's embrace again. You take this moment to fill your lungs with the tasty fresh air. You pivot to look at another mountain. This mountain is a shade of grey and blues. A fluffy grey and white cloud floats barely above the top of the mountain. They seem to be kissing one another. You imagine being on top of that mountain. You would be in a fog as you become one with the cloud. You would feel light and damp at the same time. You take in another deep breath as you picture becoming one with the cloud. Exhaling slowly you turn to look at the mountain with snow on its peak. Imagining you are on that mountain, you want to shiver. You bring your attention back to the moment and the sun is growing hot. The top of your head grows quite warm. The heat travels down your body. It is felt from your gut to your appendages. Content doesn't even begin to describe what you are feeling right now. Nothing has ever felt so peaceful. Each breath you take carries the sun's warming glow. It is traveling through your blood vessels.

You start to feel slightly sleepy. You sit on a grey rock, immediately noticing how warm it is from the sun. You close your eyes and feel at one with nature. You are grounded. The only thoughts in your mind are that of the warmth, the connection to the earth, and the sounds of the birds in the distance. You breathe deeply and feel completely whole. Joy is what you feel.

CHAPTER FOUR

You're My Obsession

I have a long-term relationship with addiction. My anorexia started when I was nine years old. There was an incident that happened just before the eating disorder came to fruition. My neighbor who was a couple years older than me took advantage of me. I was so young and naive I thought I was pregnant. I could not deal with my thoughts of guilt. "My mother is going to kill me," is all I could think about. "Why did I let this happen to me?" I did not want to get older. The boobs that I developed had to go. I wanted to go back and be the Barbie-playing child again. I did continue with playing with my dolls and My Little Pony. It did not feel the same. It felt like I was just faking it. I was almost a teenager, and from the movies I had seen I knew that sex was pretty much expected. I did not like it one bit. I knew that by restricting my eating I could lose the fat that I did not want to have, perhaps I could hold onto my childhood for that much longer.

As I started to restrict my eating, it quickly became an obsession. I felt like I was in control. I just wanted to be seen as the skinny kid I always had been. It was a game to pretend like I was eating, but I was just feeding the family dog most of the time. The pain in my stomach just reminded me that I was a bad person and I deserved it (later on I realized this was a feeling of anxiety and not hunger pains; hunger pains were the stabbing pains that would sometimes wake me up at night). The pain was going to kill the baby I imagined was growing within me. I needed an escape and through restricting my caloric intake I had found a way to distract myself.

I would think about food all day long. I loved sweets; I would restrict meals so I could continue to eat dessert. I knew that sweets would probably make me fat, but I justified that the sugar was filling up the empty hole that had developed within me. I wasn't the best anorexic at first. I was binging on sweets whenever I could. I wasn't dropping weight like I had wanted to. My boobs were only getting bigger. I knew it was because of the sugary delights I was consuming (the thought of going through puberty to cause changes never came across my mind). I needed to cut out the food that made my hollowness go away. This was difficult for me to do. I no longer had what I relied on to feel a temporary sense of being whole. I was fairly miserable for the years between the age of eleven through thirteen. I wasn't eating much, how did I get up to ninety-five pounds? I felt like I couldn't do anything right.

At the age of fourteen was when I became an expert at anorexia. My family had moved from Colorado to Maine. I needed a fresh start. I needed to be the skinny girl. This is how I was seen when I was eight. I needed that identity to define me. If I am not thin, I do not exist. I started to exercise a lot and was only eating low fat foods. I was able to at least maintain my weight at ninety-five pounds even as I grew taller. I wanted to shed a few more of those pounds though as there were other skinny girls I had to compete with. I would look at myself and think I was fat. I needed to work fast if I wanted to try and be the thin one at the school. I constantly thought, "They cannot steal my identity, those fucking bitches. I am the thin one."

I ended up at an eating disorders clinic just after I turned fifteen. It was great. I got hints from other women as to how to lose weight. I refused to eat at the clinic because in my opinion, I was not the thinnest there. I just ended up with a feeding tube and an extended stay. I couldn't wait to get out to drop the pounds yet again. I would be damned if I was going to go back to school as the fattest girl there.

When I got home after my six week stay, I started to exercise even more than I had before. I would pretend to drink my Carnation Instant Breakfast that was "prescribed" to me. I would make it in front of my parents and take a few sips to show them I was following with the recovery program. I would then dump out the rest of the drink. I had to have weekly weigh-ins at the program's outpatient doctor's office. I would drink tons of water to show that I was maintaining my weight. Eventually the water trick was not enough as the numbers on the scale were going down. I would tie weights around my abdomen and would hold the Jonny in a way that they would not be seen. I thought I was brilliant.

I was caught with my trick and the nurse practitioner was less than pleased with me. She threatened to report this to my parents, and I was forced to have a real weight taken. I immediately burst into tears. I was so mad at her for this. "How could she betray me? I need my identity. Why would she take who I am away from me? My parents are going to be so disappointed in me if the bitch reports my trick. I am a failure. I cannot get fat. My parents will be watching me eat now and probably will limit my exercise time. If I am not thin, then I do not know who I am." I did gain pity from my nurse as I was bawling my eyes out and was verbalizing how sorry I was and how sick I was and I couldn't help it. I don't think she reported anything to my parents as there was no "talk" about it. I decided to become very secretive with my exercise. I started to take several Sudafed at night, so I would wake up at three in the morning and I could at least do quiet exercise like crunches and working with my five pound weights. I was so angry that I had to do this. I needed to be thin. Why couldn't anyone see that was my identity? Everyone telling me that I needed to gain weight was out to destroy me. I couldn't look at myself as I saw this large, hideous beast. I tried to vomit after I ate, but my body does not like throwing up very much so I had to stick to exercising whenever I could get away with it.

My teenage years were consumed by my desire to be thin. The couple of friends I had, said I was thin but I did not believe them. If I was not the thinnest person at the school, I was fat. To this day, I am not sure, I may have been the thinnest girl at school, but who knows? Body dysmorphia is very real. I have never shaken body dysmorphia. I still look at people and think I wish I could be that thin. However, they are wishing they could be as thin as me. It takes a side-by-side comparison for me to re-alize I am a bit smaller. Body dysmorphia is more difficult to get past than having an eating disorder.

I did end up back in the hospital when I was seventeen as I had gotten down to eighty-five pounds. This was at the medical facility where the eating disorders clinic was. My parents' insur-ance would not cover another stay at the eating disorders pro-gram. My room was directly in front of the nurses' station. This stay was very boring as I was just in a hospital bed and could only go to the free group offered once a week. I did have a bunch of homework that I was able to keep up on. One assignment for film class was to write a 150 page screenplay. I was the only per-son in the whole class that actually completed the assignment. My passion for writing and the need to keep busy made the as-signment easy.

Although I was on the hospital side of things, I was still there to be monitored on my food intake. I was so upset about need-ing to eat three meals and have Carnation Instant Breakfast. I would dump out the Carnation and whatever food I was able to conceal in a napkin in the toilet when the nurses and psych techs were otherwise occupied. I might be ninja-like when I sneak up on someone with my quiet footsteps, but when it came to hid-ing the discarding of my food I was easily caught. I would then be watched while I was eating. I loathed it with a passion.

I struggled with my eating disorder until I turned twenty-one. I would have constant internal battles of wanting to be healthy and not obsess, to wanting to starve myself to death. In college, I had to see the doctor at the clinic fairly regularly as I was constant-ly getting sick due to a lowered immune system. As my weight was low with each visit, she said she wanted me to come in reg-ularly to monitor my weight. I also spoke of the severe depres-sion I was going through. I was a total mess, but I could not get out of my own way. The doctor eventually prescribed me Paxil.

Paxil caused me to gain a bunch of weight. I am sure the doc-tor knew this so that was why it was prescribed. I hated myself for the weight gain. I had to do something. I started to practice purging. Eventually, I was able to purge; because I could purge, I decided I could binge eat low-fat candy and ice cream. I was probably eating five thousand, high sugar, low fat calories a day. In my mind, I could justify it as it was low fat, and I could puke up some of the calories.

I transferred to Fordham University for spring semester 1995 when I was nineteen. I had wanted to get into film at the time and my other university had creative writing but not film. I tried to focus on my studies, but my binging and purging became a huge obsession for me. I had a hard time concentrating on anything else. At the rate I was going, I was probably going to get B's and C's for the semester. I would try and focus on other things rather than food. For whatever reason, I thought I could get into modeling. I am not sure why I had thought this. I was only five-five and weighed around one hundred eighteen pounds at this time. A few months prior, I was ninety-two pounds. Stupid Paxil and my switch from anorexia to being a terrible bulimic. The agent had said I was attractive enough; I just had to pay for some photos and he would see if he could get me work. I was so naive I actually did this. I did not see it for the obvious scam it was. I know a part of me thought it seemed crazy for me to have to pay for my own pictures and then maybe be considered for a local ad. I guess when it comes down to it, I was seeking validity that I was not hideous. The attempt to be a model did help reduce my obsession with binging. I tried to stop binging, so I could drop the pounds. I had also gotten off of Paxil and my binging episodes went from multiple times a day to about five days a week. My weight was decreasing very slowly.

I met a guy, probably in his late twenties, who also wanted to be a model. He said that I was hot. Even though I knew I was fat, he said I had an amazing body. My weight had gone to my ass and tits, I guess the good places, but I did not look at it this way. I liked the attention he was giving me. We went out for coffee together. I could tell he wanted to have sex with me. I was still all caught up in my nine year old experience and definitely did not want to have sex with him. I just met him for Christ's sake. I told him flat out, "I'm laying my cards on the table, I am no going to have sex with you." Did I mention that I'm naive? I thought this was going to be enough so he would just stick to making out. I ended up inviting him to my dorm. If you look in the dictionary under the word naive, you would see my picture. He forced me to perform oral on him even though I was saying no and crying the whole time. He kept telling me to stop being such a baby. He probably would have raped me vaginally as well if I hadn't started my menstrual cycle. I felt so worthless at this time. I just wanted to kill myself to escape from the pain. I spent a night in a Manhattan psych ward. I ended up dropping out of Fordham and went back to Maine. I was extremely downtrodden. I felt completely hopeless.

My therapist had suggested I try out an eating disorders clinic in Philadelphia to help with my eating disorder, which now bounced from bulimic episodes to restrictive episodes. I was at the clinic for a couple of weeks, but it did not help me much. Again, it was another situation where I felt like I was too fat for the program and I loathed myself for being an incompetent bulimic. It felt like I was such a failure. I knew I had to go back to just restricting my intake and hopefully it would be easier as I was prescribed Prozac at the clinic. Prozac was not known for weight gain.

I lost many months at this time as I was not in school and I wasn't working. I was miserable and now obsessing about food and exercise was not helping me stuff my feelings away. I ended up in a mental hospital twice during this time as I couldn't get suicide off my mind. I had been able to drop quite a few pounds and was down to one hundred and two pounds. I could tolerate being at this weight; I was an adult after all. I still wanted to drop more weight, but it was hard to do so. I had given up on life and my identity of being thin was no longer in my mind. I didn't deserve an identity.

I did eventually go back to school. At this time, I decided to start dating women. The thought hadn't really occurred to me that I liked woman as well as men until I was eighteen. I should have known when I was younger. I was obsessed with Jodie Foster when I was a kid and my walls were always filled with pictures of actresses I thought were pretty. I did not decide to explore this part of myself until I turned twenty-one. At this time, I was able to let go of my eating disorder. I still would think I was fat and restrict on occasion, but it was no longer my obsession. I am sure that smoking weed was also a factor in me letting go from my obsession with my caloric intake.

For a few years I was a pothead. I wouldn't say it was an addiction for me, but I would go crazy if all of my suppliers were out of weed. I started drinking at this time as I was no longer concerned about caloric intake. Alcohol, at first, was a temporary escape for me. It wasn't until I was in my mid-twenties that I needed it to escape from reality. One lousy summer job, and alcohol was my savior.

I used alcohol a lot through my adult life. I never drank when I was pregnant, but I drank a lot at all other times. When I was pregnant, I temporarily filled my void by being a workaholic. I wouldn't say my alcoholism got out of control until I had my third child and was in my early thirties.

My emotions have always been so intense and alcohol was the only thing that could numb me out. I also felt this constant pain of emptiness in my chest and alcohol would fill my empty shell. I actually wished I had started to binge drink at a younger age. I felt it would have gotten me through the ups and downs of my teenage years. Alcohol was not an enemy; it was a friend. Hell, alcohol was a lover. I thought I was drinking as much as everyone else, and therefore I was not an alcoholic.

At first, I was able to refrain from drinking on Mondays and Tuesdays. I would think about drinking on these days but forced myself not to. I mean, I didn't want to become an alcoholic after all. I knew I had an addictive personality and that is why I had never tried any hard drugs like crack or heroin. I knew if I could refrain from drinking for two days out of the week that would stop me from becoming addicted to alcohol. These months with this experiment did not last long.

When I worked at a job I enjoyed, it was easier for me to stick with just two or three beers a night. I would be able to relax and enjoy my evening. As long as things were going well in my marriage, this was something I could stick with, two beers a night Monday through Thursday and several more Friday through Sunday. I had it under control. I found something that helped me and it wasn't hurting anyone.

When I started to work for the phone company was when things started to go downhill quickly for me. If I had known it was a sales job from the get-go, I would have never taken the job. I did not learn it was a sales job until halfway through my training. At this point in time however, I had heard that in a couple of years I would be making thirty plus dollars an hour. I did not even get paid that much as an Ed Tech on overtime. I had to stick it out to help pull my family out of debt and have enough money to spend on the things we needed.

As I figured, I was horrible at sales. I always saw sales people as vultures. I know this is not true of sales people, but it was my opinion. I just had a really hard time with tricking people into buying what they did not need. I was completely honest about the terms of service and early termination fees. I would even explain that tax would add another twenty or so dollars to the price quote I had given. Several of my coworkers would gloss over the terms and say plus tax rather than explaining how high the tax actually was. I would get the customer back questioning why the bill was so high. I would explain it to them. They would get really mad at me for my honesty and ask why the other representative never went over any of this. It was a union job, so I couldn't throw anyone under the bus, although I wished I could. I would have to make up some lame ass excuse and I would be raging on the inside.

When I got home, I would bitch about my day to Jason. I always had a beer in hand while I was doing this. The alcohol released my pent up stress. If Jason told me to calm down as I was talking about work, I would just drink more. I was working at a job I hated to be able to support the family as I was the breadwinner and Jason was the stay-at-home parent. If Jason wouldn't let me be animated with my feelings about the day, I at least had alcohol to take me away.

My drinking kept increasing as the same amount of alcohol was not having the same effect on me. I was only drinking four or so beers a night, so I had it covered. I was just drinking enough to get buzzed and numb out. There is nothing wrong with wanting to numb out. With my job, I needed it or I would have gone completely insane. I was just doing what I had to. There was no way that I was an alcoholic. I just liked drinking. I figured I could stop at anytime if I wanted to. The thing was I did not want to. Why would I give up an escape from all of my feelings? I was able to go to work everyday and still read to my children at night. As long as I was doing what was needed to be done, I was fine.

In 2014, I was concerned that I might actually be an alcoholic. I decided I would go the month of May with only drinking on special occasions so I could lower my tolerance level and prove to everyone, including myself, that I was not addicted. I did refrain from drinking for a few days. I could not get the obsession of drinking out of my head. I decided that as I was not going through a detox, I was not an alcoholic. I couldn't keep the obsessive thoughts out of my head, so I went right back to drinking again. I might as well, as I just proved I was not an alcoholic.

When the union went on strike in October 2014, I continued to drink as much as I had been but this time I was drinking nasty-ass forties. It was affordable, and I was able to reduce the stress of being on strike. The strike lasted until February 2015. One hundred thirty-one days I was on strike, the longest in telco history. I think my biggest relief was that I could go back to drinking good beer. I hated my job but loved the money.

My spiral into the abyss had started. I would keep consuming more and more beer or vodka. I did not want to get a buzz anymore. I wanted to get blackout and pass out drunk. I loathed my job and the life I was living. When I would black out, I would enjoy not remembering a thing from the night before. I just wish it would have drowned out the phone calls I took the previous day. I was really trying to escape from work. I just wish I could pick and chose what I remembered or not. I would go into work hungover on a daily basis. I was still making it in to work, so I was fine. If I was an alcoholic, I at least, was a high-functioning alcoholic.

From November of 2016 to November of 2017, I was out of control. I had started an online affair with a man. I did not see that this was a problem. I thought it was innocent. It was destroying my marriage. No matter how many times I was screamed at about it, I would not stop. I felt obsessed and I could not control myself. My head was so foggy that I had a hard time in seeing error to my ways. I could not stop, so I would drink more and continue with my online flirtation. It made me feel good as I was desired by someone other than Jason. It's another addiction of mine to be lusted after by different people. I thought that as long as I felt good it was all that mattered.

As time went on, I did feel some guilt from this affair. I would try to justify in my mind that I needed it to survive. I justified that because it was not physical, it was not that bad. The guilt would still jab at me no matter what type of bullshit I was feeding myself. I thought more beer was what I needed. The only way to escape from my thoughts was to drown them. When six pounders was not getting me pass out drunk, I had to limit my intake of food. I was still trying to prove to myself that I was not an alcoholic. As long as I could stick with the equivalency of eight beers a night Monday through Thursday and up to thirteen beers on the weekend, I was still fine. I knew this was a ridiculous thing to think, but it was the story I told myself. Deep down, I knew I was an alcoholic, but I did not want to admit it to myself.

I pretty much stopped eating and just consumed my calories in alcohol. I had gotten down to eighty-nine pounds. My old friend anorexia helped me with this. I liked being thin again but would hate the fact that I would be in major pain if I sat longer than ten minutes. I did not care though, as long as I was thin and able to pass out after my eight beers, I was doing fine.

I knew I wasn't fine, though. I knew that I was an alcoholic. I kicked myself for falling into this addiction. I wanted to be able to just go back and be happy with two beers a night. I was making very poor decisions. I still cannot believe I threatened to kill the management team on social media. This was early August of 2017. If I only had two beers, I would have known to watch what I wrote and refrain from those types of comments. I did post my threat of bringing in a gun to shoot management in a closed, union-member-only page, but I knew that whatever you write on social media can come back and haunt you. It really did haunt me. It was so hard to sit in a room with a union steward and two managers. The conversation was so accusatory. I felt like a peanut shell without its nuts. I was on the brink of tears the whole time. I explained that I did not remember what I wrote and I did not own a gun so I would never hunt down management. I was asked question after question. I finally admitted that I was an alcoholic and was feeling highly suicidal. I was still put on indefinite suspension, but they wanted me to get help and not just go home and get drunk. It was so embarrassing to be walked out of the office by management. The rumor mill started right away. "Hot off the press, Kirsten was walked out, she probably will get fired for threatening to kill people. Hopefully she is fired so that whack job will never come back." I don't know exactly what they had said, but it would have been along those lines.

I ended up at Spring Harbor. I was told by my psychiatrist there that I should just stop drinking. Drinking seemed to be the source of all of my problems. All I had to do was quit and I would feel better. I tried to not drink after I got out eight days later. I did not make it long until my feelings were overwhelming and I started to sneak drinking. It was really hard for me to pretend I wasn't drunk so I was caught easily. Jason started to buy me a six pack of Michelob Ultra and that was what I would be limited to a day. I would buy vodka and hide it as I usually needed more than the six beers. I had participated in partial hospital. It was highly recommended to be sober during the intensive program.

I was drunk on most nights after the program, as it delved into talking about feelings I did not want to get into. I definitely did not get much out of the program this first time through. My drinking had a lot to do with that. I just could not remain sober on my own. It was easy in the hospital because I had no choice. Okay, I shouldn't lie; it was easier in the hospital but I was highly anxious and emotional without my drink.

I kept falling deeper into my addiction. I did not know how to quit on my own so I gave up. I might as well just keep drinking myself stupid. My oldest son had started to feel highly suicidal and made a suicidal gesture in September. I knew it was because of me. He is *my* son. He unfortunately got the depression issues from me. I knew I had to do something. People told me to go to AA. I was not thrilled with the idea of going to AA, so I did not do this. I did decide at the end of October that I probably should go to rehab as I was only making matters worse and nothing was improving for me. I still obsessed about suicide on a daily basis. The one rehab I was going to be all set to go to ended up rejecting me as I didn't weigh enough in their opinion. They referred me to an eating disorders clinic and I lost my shit. I had learned this information on my lunch break at work. I had to tell management what happened and needed to go home sick as I could not think clearly. I was a crying mess. They told me to get ahold of the EAP (Employee Assistance Program) social worker. They said that she might have suggestions for me. The social worker had helped me and I ended up on a detox floor of St. Mary's, a hospital that specialized in mental illness and addiction, on November 3. They were the ones who referred me to Crossroads, the thirty-day rehab I started on November 8. I went straight from St. Mary's to Crossroads so I wouldn't be tempted to drink and decide not to go.

Crossroads was an excellent program for a woman in the very early stages of recovery. I was a bit obstinant at first. I did not like the fact that we were only going to AA and NA meetings. The meetings seemed cultish to me. I am an atheist, so I had a hard time with the fact that I just needed to give up my will to a magical Tooth Fairy. In my mind it seemed this ridiculous. "Oh please, Tooth Fairy, please help show me a way to remain sober, I don't have a tooth for you but will you help anyway?" So, there was my obstinance in action. I do not have issues with others having higher powers or following organized religion, but it is not my thing.

I knew that the twelve-step programs have helped out millions of people, but I was just not one of them. I learned about SMART and we went to one of the groups with the rehab as I said that it would be helpful to me. The younger ladies at the rehab would not shut up as to how much they hated SMART as it was like doing a clinical and learning stuff. I was like, well I do not believe in the twelve-step programs and self management and science is what works for me. They gave me a hard time about it until the end of my stay.

About halfway through rehab, my head started to feel a lot clearer. I had no idea how cloudy everything was when my brain was sitting in alcohol. I also was eating three healthy meals a day and was putting weight on. I started to grow at this time. The clinicians there told me that they could see a huge improvement and I had turned a one-eighty. I agreed. I said I felt like a different person and now all I had to do was to figure out who I was. For what ever reason, I temporarily had brain damage. I forgot that I have never known who I was.

I had to fight off cravings multiple times a day when I got out of rehab. The pain in my chest had returned. I used a lot of distraction and avoidance strategies. I was also going to SMART twice a week. I would constantly do cost-benefit analyses to help keep me focused on my sobriety. I did like having a clear mind and not waking up hungover everyday. I also found out that I had not become a bad driver after all; I just didn't drive well when I was buzzed or hungover. I kept the prize of sobriety in my mind. It was very difficult to not give into a craving. Every time I did not give in I became stronger. I treated it like a game and I was winning. I felt strong until my mental health issues decided to kick in full time in February of 2018. At this time, my cravings only occurred a few times a week. I was back to feeling suicidal yet again. I could have just gone back to drinking, but I had worked so hard and I told myself I would get through a year of sobriety. I think it was out of stubbornness, I did not pick up a drink every time my emotions were overwhelming.

In March 2018 I started to obsess about suicide. I did a lot of research on the internet for various ways to kill myself and the effectiveness. Without an addiction, I had felt lost. My new addiction was to plan out my death. This has been a major focus for me in 2018. I will get more into my suicidality in another chapter.

On November 19, 2018, (I'm writing this paragraph November 20th) I did have a slip with alcohol. I figured I had gone over a year without drinking and maybe I could moderate myself. I was completely wrong. Once the beer touched my lips, I had to drain all of the bottles as quickly as I could. I should have done a cost-benefit analysis before I made the decision to drink. It was almost like the year of sobriety I had gone out the window. I loved drinking for the first hour. I felt so free. I was able to hide from my emotions for a short stint. However, it was only for a moment. I got tearful as I continued to drink as I am an alcoholic and the three IPA's I was planning on holding myself to was not enough. The hangover I have reminds me why I need to remain strong. I'm definitely not perfect. I did learn from the slip. I learned that I will never be able to moderate, and I need to stay away from alcohol. I learned that the glorification I gave to alcohol on November 19th was false. I am not proud of myself for having the slip, but it happened and I needed to be honest with myself. I wasn't going to tell anyone but I ended up telling a lot of people what I did. It helped me to not keep it as a secret. I now know that drinking isn't the cure I had remembered it was. Alcohol is a quick fix, and its only lasting effects are the shame and the pounding in my head. I will remember this the next time I am tempted.

Oops, another update. What I thought was just going to be a slip with alcohol turned into a hardcore relapse. I ended up drinking 8–15 beers a day from November 21st through December

4th. I am writing this paragraph now on December 23rd. I am currently in a crisis stabilization unit (CSU) after I had several lengthy stays in the emergency department, as well as on the psych ward of a hospital. The positive of being institutionalized is that I have been away from alcohol, and I will hopefully remain sober once I leave the CSU. I did fall right back into my alcoholism and this time I felt like I was worse than before. I would wake up at six a.m. and have a beer in my hand by six-thirty. I was a complete mess the thirteen days. I became very suicidal and ended up at three different emergency departments.

I really should have known on the nineteenth that my slip was not going to be just a one-day event. Relapse technically happens well before you pick up that first drink or drug. I started this relapse process in October but never caught my warning signs. This is something I should have noticed. I almost think I did notice the warning signs of relapse but chose to ignore them. I had stopped following my recipe for recovery. I was no longer exercising everyday, and I was not eating healthy meals. At least one meal a day for me would be peanuts, Craisins, and M&M's. I would eat a large bowl of ice-cream and have at least twenty fun-sized candy bars. I was compulsive overeating to try and tone down the anxiety I was feeling. I was highly anxious and depressed and never caught the fact that I was relapsing towards drinking. I truly do hope that I will not drink again. Relapse is a part of recovery. It's too bad mine was after a year. I had made a bet with myself to be sober for a year and I just met that goal barely. I have to remain strong. Knowing I had gone a year means I can succeed. I can do it again. I just need to keep up with the activities that helped me stay sober in the first place.

There was one activity in rehab that I found was psychoscribble worthy. It was writing a letter to my addiction. As I mentioned at the very beginning of the book, I was not going to edit my psychoscribble pieces as to me I find it more authentic. I had to write this letter in my journal at rehab. It was December 1, 2017 that I wrote the piece. When I went to type it into my computer, I tried to keep it word for word. I did not do that one hundred percent as I have horrible handwriting and I had to guess on a few of the things I wrote. I, of course, wrote my letter to my addiction as if I were writing to a person. Again, this is what works best for me. I was honest in the letter and admitted that I loved my addiction, but it was hurting me too much. I suggest that if you decide to write to your addiction no matter what it is, you just have to be completely honest with your thoughts and emotions. It is through honesty that clarity can be seen.

I have included a sample of a cost-benefit analysis. I did mine based on the alcohol addiction. A cost-benefit analysis can be used on any unwanted behavior. I love it as once I see something in black and white and I was the one who created it, it makes much more sense for me to choose sobriety. I've included my recipe for recovery as well as a mock chain analysis of what led me to picking up that drink on November 19th. Just for fun, I ended with a poem about my relapse.

12/1/17
Dear Alcoholism,

Do you seriously think I have forgotten about you? How could I ever forget? I dream about you often still. You are constantly showing up in my mind, a whirlwind sweeping me afloat. I can still hear you whisper to me, begging for my forgiveness.

You were there for me when I needed help. You made this socially awkward girl come to life and shine. Everyone hated me, but not you. You warmed me from the inside when I was feeling hollow and empty. When I was filled, I was funny and socially accepted. You gave me that power.

You may have saved my life several times. I felt so low in my shell, death was the thought on my mind. Again, I was not loved. Everyone always leaves. I had you to give me the encouragement to move on. I was able to escape all of my thoughts of loneliness and death. You made life tolerable.

As of late, you have been pushing me into a different direction. You are telling me I should hurt myself. You are telling me that I do not deserve to live. You have brought me to the edge of a cliff and I feel like a taste of liquor will make me fall. A month ago my impulsivity was at an all time high. I am shocked that I survived.

I am mad at you for the recent burn marks on my skin. You burned me in a prominent place so all can see how crazy I am. I was blackout drunk at the time and do not know why you made me do it. I am sure you want to blame my friend Borderline Personality Disorder on that one. Perhaps it was a joint effort between the two of you. Kirsten is in la la land now, lets take advantage of that. I guess I will never know for sure as neither of you will explain it to me. You would probably just lie to me anyway. You like to lie and love it when I lie too. It's the glue that has held us together.

I am sure if you were right here with me, you would be arguing with me and throwing things into my face. You would say, take a drink, relax. You would say I am not an alcoholic. You would remind me that in my adult life I did quit drinking for my three pregnancies so I can control my liquor. I had cheated on you at that time with workaholism and compulsive over eating. You are probably still mad at me for that but I came back. I came back to you with my full heart and soul. My last ten years have been dedicated to you. You are my favorite.

Shit. Just imagining your warmth within me, I want to forgive you. There were so many good times. I feel like I need you back in my life. This was supposed to be a Dear John letter. Fuck me. Fuck you. Damn fucking feelings.

Okay, in all seriousness, I love you. I also hate you. You have caused me so much pain over these last several months. I was back to my really old patterns of suicide attempts, burning and cutting. You completely isolated me from the world. I had gone along willingly. I was ignoring everyone. You were the only one who mattered in my life. I loved the cold beer I would have as soon as I got home from work. The beer was the first thing I went to. I did not kiss my husband or talk to my kids. It was you. I was kissing you as I would down the alcohol in less than two minutes. My husband started to get jealous of our relationship. I did not care. You were the true love of my life.

As time went by, I had to keep consuming more and more alcohol to bring you to life. The warm embrace was the best feeling. The warmth was more and more difficult to gain from you in the end. I just wanted you to hold me. To numb me. To make me forget how miserable my life is.

The problem is that you changed and the escape was only for brief seconds before I would think about dying. The numbness was not doing the same thing for me. All of a sudden I was not able to run away from my emotions. I don't know why you did that to me. I kept trying and trying. I couldn't just give up.

I was crying every night and going into work hungover and miserable every day. I was a zombie not even functioning on a human level. I need to feel well again. I need to perform job better than I have been over the last several months. Don't worry, workaholism is not going to be my new lover. Trust me, babe, with that job I would never turn to workaholism. Workaholism is a lousy lover anyway. You are the one and only lover for me.

Shit, I do this with every break up. I leave the door open a crack. I am going to try to stay firm and push it closed if you do arrive. I am stronger now. I am eating healthily now. I have tools at my disposal to use. I am a different person now than the one you fell in love with. Such as you are different than the person I had originally fell in love with.

I do still love you, but you are killing me. I am going to miss the good times. I am going to grieve for this loss. You are not giving me what I need anymore, too many years of misery. This is supposed to be a goodbye not an I'll see you later moment. Goodbye, my love.

Cost-Benefit Analysis

Substance or behavior to consider is: <u>Drinking Alcohol</u>

Using or Doing

**Advantages
(benefits and rewards)**

- Numbs me out
- Dulls emotions
- It's a quick fix
- The high
- Escape
- Social
- lower inhibition

**Disadvantages
(costs and risks)**

- Hangovers
- Not remembering the night before
- Isolation/missed time with family
- Risk of driving under influence/getting arrested
- Loss of jobs
- Health problems
- Foggy brain
- Impulsive decisions easily made
- I can be a jerk when drunk
- Waking up with bruises and not knowing how they got there
- Financially expensive
- I make a fool out of myself

NOT Using or NOT Doing

Advantages
(benefits and rewards)

- I have a clear mind
- I can get in car and drive anytime
- No hangovers
- I'm not a jerk
- I'm available for family
- I can have friends as I'm available emotionally
- Saves money
- Better memory
- No lost days
- I feel accountable for my actions/no more blaming of others
- I do not scream at the top of my lungs at Jason anymore
- I am free from the obsession

Disadvantages
(costs and risks)

- I have to feel my emotions
- I have to use skills to get through
- Nothing is better for a quick fix
- I have to face reality
- Social anxiety is more pronounced
- It is a long journey to recovery

My Everyday Recipe for Recovery

- Morning exercise, stretching and cardio for at least 30 minutes a day
- Water
- Three meals a day
- Water
- Take medication as prescribed
- Water
- Dark chocolate (I like to savor it and let it melt in my mouth)
- Water
- Do something mindfully, I like to mindfully smoke a cigarette or eat something
- Water
- Use either distraction or look at my cost benefit analysis when an urge sets in
- Water
- Self-care such as washing my face with a nice product or painting my nails
- Water
- Telling myself that every minute I go without a drink is a win
- Most importantly, water, lots and lots of water

Snacks to Throw in

- Distract with a comedy
- Meditate
- Draw
- Paint
- Write
- Reach out to someone
- Go on a walk
- Spend quality time with the boys
- Bake cookies or brownies
- Clean the house (in desperate times. Desperate times call for desperate measures)

Chain Analysis for Drinking

It was not surprising that I had started my path of relapse on November 19th. I had several factors leading up to it. I had wanted to go a year of sobriety. I had reached that goal on November 4th. I was thinking that maybe I could moderate my drinking at this point. I had refrained from drinking right away though as I had already gone the year and I might as well keep it up.

The first factor leading to my drinking is the fact that I had already started to relapse. I was feeling like a dry drunk from around October going forward. I stopped following my recipe for recovery and forgot to use my cost-benefit analysis. I had become a compulsive overeater to push down my feelings of anxiety. The dead, empty pit inside of me was hungry. It was hungry for alcohol and not for candy. Yet candy is what I fed it. I got fat. I am fat. I hate being fat. I was 89 pounds when I was a heavy drinker in 2017. I thought that if I switched from sweets to alcohol I could drop the pounds once again.

The second factor is living with Amy. She had been drinking on and off herself. I had been able to refrain from drinking myself as she got buzzed and drunk for several weeks. She had an upsetting message from her soon to be ex-wife on November 19th. She had already bought one alcoholic beverage that was there when I got to her place. I flippantly said that I was upset that my last alcoholic beverage I would ever have in my life was Miller Lite. I wanted to have IPA's or vodka as my last drinks. I said lets get drunk together. I haven't had a female friend to drink with in ages, not since my early twenties. I thought it would be fun if we were drunk together. It was a lot of fun. I regretted the drinking the next morning but got right back into it on Wednesday.

Another factor was on the 19th I heard that an old friend of mine had died. Most likely he died from complications from drinking. I thought in my head maybe I could also die from complications from drinking. He was only a year older than me. So this thought plus the loss of a friend also triggered me to drink on the 19th.

My despondency of not being able to find a job yet and my anxiety of not being able to afford things soon also played a role. I felt like I cannot do anything correctly. The only thing I was ever good at in my entire life was being a drunk. I can be a lot of fun when I drink. Well, a lot of fun until the sixth or seventh beverage that is. Then I turn into an asshole. I wanted to be the fun me again. I hate being the sad and hopeless me. Drinking would be able to at least temporarily bring me back into feeling more like myself again.

It would have been extremely easy to prevent the drinking from happening. I could have just been there for Amy as a friend, and if she wanted to get drunk I could have just stayed by her side. I have been around Amy when she was drunk and I was sober so many times. It really would have been simple to just not drink. I convinced myself that drinking would be fun and it was only going to be for the one night. I really thought that was the case. I did not do a cost-benefit analysis before I said we should start drinking. I was just thinking of wanting to have fun in the moment. I also didn't think I was going to need to go back out to get more alcohol. I thought three IPA's would be enough but it wasn't; I needed shots and some lite beer as well. So, yes, Amy and I went out to the store, drunk. We could have gotten into an accident or got a DUI. This would have been a severe consequence. It did not happen though and so I think I was more likely to continue drinking again. I stayed sober on November 20th, but that has really been the only day since my binge drinking that I have been sober.

I ended up in the ED on Tuesday night as a direct result of me having half a bottle of vodka. I was extremely suicidal in my blackout drunk state. I think I took several Trazadone that night as I was missing my pills the following day. I would not have gotten super suicidal like I was if I had not been drinking. I would not have gotten kicked out of the house again if I had not been drinking. I clearly can see that drinking is not the best option for me. I keep going back to it for the fun I have at the beginning of the day. I know I lead to feeling suicidal and miserable but I just want the few minutes of peace I get in the beginning.

I am facing several consequences right now. I still drank a ton last night, November 30th. This was after a terrible conversation I had with my mother and stepfather. I was seeing if I could live with them as Amy needs to be on her own and I cannot stay here for forever. I thought about going to my mothers as I would have a bedroom with my own private bathroom. There is hot water at my mother's house. I thought it might be nice to be there as my mother wants to reconnect with me. I want to reconnect with her as well, but her sadness really rubs off on me and I grow quite despondent. I knew this was going to be an issue, but I thought I would ask as Jason is not letting me home anytime soon after Tuesday night and my suicidal gesture. I was going to deal with the situation the best I could and it would probably involve a lot of isolation. My mother and stepfather do not like that idea. So, I had a couple of IPA's, went to SMART, and then pounded the other four on an empty stomach. I wanted to kill myself. I did not have enough pills on me to do so. I had considered driving drunk to get to a store to by pills and then more alcohol and then to a hotel. Amy helped me get into bed instead. I was super drunk and would have gotten into an accident for sure. I had driven drunk several times over the last ten days, but I was only going short distances so I was never caught to get a DUI.

The only way to have prevented myself from falling down this path would have been me doing a cost-benefit analysis. I did not do this. I was looking for the quick fix high and did not consider long term complications. I do have long-term complications as I am kicked out of my house yet again. I am not going to be surprised if it turns out to be long term. I am not going to be surprised if he will end up divorcing me at this rate. I went back to drinking and I really don't seem to have any plans to quit soon. I know I need to do this and maybe I will get through today of being sober. I have done it in the past, and it was extremely difficult and uncomfortable. There isn't any reason why I won't be able to go through this difficulty again now. I did it before. I think it will be the first couple of weeks that will be really hard and then it will get easier. I do have a year of sobriety under my belt, and I learned different coping skills. I just need to bring them out again.

Last Dance

Stairway to Heaven
The speakers have spoken
Near the coats
I blend in
I stand
I watch
So far away
Five clock shadow
Leather over white T
Like a zooming of a lens
You are here
Kissing my hand
Asking
One last dance
It's been a year
You look good
Knees shake
Kissing my cheek
One last dance
I want to run
Kissing my neck
One last dance
Words flow off
Your tongue
My mouth chases
The promise
Just one last dance
Rumpled sheets
Explosion in my mind
Glance at watch
Days vanished
Dry mouth
Nausea
Pounding construction

Brain hurts
You smile
You beckon
You need me close
You have me
It's been a year
I turn away
Tears flowing
It was supposed to be
One last dance

CHAPTER FIVE

To Be or Not To Be

I have quite the long history with suicidal ideation. I have definitely gone years without thinking about suicide. Once she whispers in my ear, I end up becoming obsessed with suicide. The smallest thing can set me off kilter, and I am researching ways that I can kill myself online. Here in 2018, suicidal thoughts and actions have made a home. I have had several hospitalizations and have been out of work for most of the year due to this. It is my obsession. Dr. Price told me I had to take suicide off the table back in July. I have since made a nearly fatal attempt in September 2018. I cannot understand why everyone thinks I should live. I am not contributing anything to society, and I am a complete bore. Through a couple of psychoscribble activities, I have seen reasons to live but my intense pain sometimes takes over and I still seek death.

Dr. Price wondered why I would feel suicidal and end up in the hospital after a seemingly meaningless event. He couldn't understand why I wanted to die because there was construction going on while I was at work. This is just one example of my many attempts this year alone. He asked me to explain to him what exactly is going on in my brain to want to jump to committing suicide so easily. This is how I explained it to him in psychoscribble form July 2018:

"For me, it's a like a game of Jenga. I do start off with a nice solid base, maybe missing a piece or two. This foundation is just above my obsessive thoughts of suicide. Everyday life events remove the pieces from the lower levels and add them to the top. After several moves, my base is no longer strong. The building is top heavy and the next negative event could cause the blocks to tumble. When the blocks tumble, that is when I turn

to suicide. The act of suicide is not a far reach from my fingertips. If I do not seek out help, I might end up dead or even worse, brain damaged.

I do have a lot of coping skills, and therefore I have a nice solid base. The times the base is completely solid is after there has been positive events in my life. I usually had a fairly solid base after Partial Hospital and Spring Harbor Hospital respites. My foundation after my thirty days at Crossroads, my rehab, was extremely solid. When I came across negative stressors, the middle pieces were pulled instead of the bottom pieces. Of course, two weeks after I was out of rehab, I had started to pull from the lower pieces after what I perceived was an extremely negative event.

I needed to continue my treatment for my recovery as the alcohol cravings were severe. The staff at Crossroads told me I would benefit most from completing the six-week IOP program after my residential treatment was finished. I started the program the Monday after I got out of rehab. I gained a lot from the three-hour days where I learned many new skills. I was gladly participating in the program. I soaked up every new suggestion determined that I was going to be successful in my recovery. On day nine of the program, I ended up receiving a call about my short-term disability. The person told me she would love to approve me being out of work for the six weeks, however per rules from my employer I had to have a psychiatrist co-sign the paperwork. Crossroads does not have a psychiatrist and I was still on a waiting list for one, so I had to suddenly go back to work the very next day.

However, I still did not fall at this time. I focused on my sobriety. This kept me busy enough that the voice that cries out for me to kill myself became almost silent. I continued the best I could with playing the middle pieces from there on out. Eventually, I ran out of stable middle pieces and had to grab from the bottom. It only took a couple of plays, and I crashed again, hard. Something took ahold of me with this crash in April. I pulled myself out of the rubble and rebuilt the structure with the pieces that were strong enough to survive. This time, my base was not a strong one. The base is missing multiple pieces. I was starting with a weak foundation.

So, as you can see. It is very reasonable to have negative events add to the already unstable mind and end up figuring out that death is the only way out of the pain and frustration. This is especially true when you

know you are going to keep failing over and over. It is certainly some-
thing I am always thinking about. I asked my only two friends I have
right now, who also have BPD, and they agree with me, suicide is rea-
sonable if a major stressor such as loud noise at work occurs. Negativity
stacked onto negativity leads to wanting to complete suicide. You could
also look at it as potential energy that turns into kinetic energy. It is very
hard to stop the idea and calm the mind. It's as if suicide has become a
part of my life."

I still truly believe that I am playing Jenga on a regular basis here. As I am writing these words in October 2018, I have not made any attempts since my near fatal one in September 2018. I have thought about suicide a lot since that time, however. I had gathered a bunch of pills that I was going to consume with alcohol at a hotel. My plan was to get into the bathtub when I got extremely drowsy so I would sink into the water to die. It seems like it would be a sure thing. Jason stopped me from leaving the house, and he got rid of the pills. I still sit here and do research on what pill and alcohol combination will actually kill me.

Now in early November 2018, I do not have health insurance and I cannot afford a visit to the ER, so I would have to make sure that I would actually die if I make an attempt. I know this is clouded thinking, but it is how I feel. So far, I have been good and have made phone calls to my psychiatrist when I am feeling deeply suicidal and I think I will act on it. I have also reached out to Jason when this occurs. I feel like they are giving me a bit more oxygen for my deep plunge, but diving is the direction I am headed and it feels like it's just a matter of time before I end up running out of air.

After I started drinking again in November 2018, I was running dangerously low on oxygen. I stopped reaching out for help as the alcohol increased my impulsivity ten fold. I am writing this paragraph in mid December 2018. As drinking lowers my impulse control, I have ended up in the emergency department four times in a matter of a few weeks. I currently feel overwhelmed about my current situation. I do not have a place I can live at as

Jason and Amy kicked me out do to the recent suicidal gestures. I do not have a job and I have been waiting for Social Security to deny my request for Social Security Disability Insurance (SSDI) so I could appeal the decision ASAP. I have been told by many people that everyone tends to be denied on the first SSDI application. They say that SSDI is usually denied on the second application as well. I was told to expect needing to fill out a third application and at this time I should likely be approved. I have a lot hovering above me. I cannot see that my life will get any better at this time. A life worth living seems so far fetched. The demands have been actively running in my mind.

My suicidal ideation started when I was thirteen years old. I was abandoned by all of my friends and the internal pain was too much to bear. I just made a half-hearted attempt at this time. I thought that taking more of the recommended dose of Sudafed in a twenty-four hour period and lightly cutting my wrists was going to do it. Cut me some slack, this was the days before the internet. I still thought of dying daily. I was hoping I would die in a car accident. I just wished I could close my eyes and sleep forever. Perhaps I am an atheist now as I used to say at night, "God, please let me die in my sleep. Please, God." As I obviously didn't die, I figured a higher power did not exist.

My thoughts of suicide subsided a bit during high school. I would find ways to hurt myself such as cutting or taking a lot more Tylenol than I was supposed to. I did not make a suicide attempt in high school. I had the thoughts, but I never acted on them. My high school years weren't too bad overall. I attribute a lot of this to my best friend, Shannon. She has been my savior. I am sure I had a bit of codependency on Shannon but our relationship was always strong.

Once I got to college, I started to obsess about death again. I was hoping I could starve myself to death or somehow will myself to death. Of course neither of these options would work. I did have an overdose when I was twenty and going to school in Manhattan. I stayed overnight in the psych ward of a nearby hospital. I ended up dropping out of school and I moved back to Maine. I had several hospitalizations that year. Suicide had let herself be known, and I wanted to follow her down the path towards peace. It took a good year for me to stop having the obsessive thoughts of suicide.

I was still performing self harm during this time for various reasons. I did it to not feel so empty and zombie-like. I did it for a quick rush. I harmed myself to feel pain other than the one I felt on the inside. My twenties and thirties basically played out like this: I might have some suicidal thoughts and a couple of actions, but I wasn't a slave to suicidal thinking at that time. I am sure my heavy drinking probably stuffed the feelings of wanting to die away. I know alcohol is a depressant, but it masked my feelings and got me to pass out before my suicidal ideation could grasp her nails into my back.

It wasn't until I was forty and my alcoholism got really severe that my suicidal thoughts started right back up again. I would scream out that I wanted to die and I needed something to kill myself with. I put Jason through hell. He had to take me to the ER multiple times in 2017. Some of the times I was actually able to take a bunch of pills before going to the hospital, other times I was brought there before I could injure myself. I know I was hurting Jason and the kids. I just needed to escape from my pain. The alcohol was not doing it for me anymore. The alcohol started to increase my impulsivity around hurting myself. I had terrible ideas like hanging myself with a bathrobe belt. Suicidal Ideation was begging me to follow her. I tried to follow but wasn't successful as I would always make a huge screaming and crying scene before I would grab the utility knife or a bunch of pills. I was very vocal as to what I wanted to do and then would end up in the ER. I was tired of the multiple ER visits and decided that I needed to check myself into rehab in November 2017.

After I was sober for four months, my anxiety and fears took over. I started to contemplate suicide as, here I was sober for a length of time, and I felt even more miserable than I had when I was drinking. I know the easiest thing would have been to go back to drinking again to hide from my empty, painful emotions.

I was too stubborn and determined to go back to drinking. Instead I just obsessed about suicide. I spent a lot of time online researching various ways to kill myself. I would plan out when I would do it. I really hated my job at the phone company, so the ideal spot would be in the woods adjoining the parking lot at work. I finally got a psychiatrist in March 2018. I asked her for three months worth of pills so I had something I could use to sedate myself with before I tied a chicken roasting bag around my head to die of carbon monoxide poisoning. The doctor did not know me well enough to know that more that a seven day supply of pills would be abused. I did not end up working with this psychiatrist for very long as I had a couple of in-patient and out-patient hospitalizations just after I started to work with her. When I got out of my three week hospitalization at Spring Harbor in May 2018, I was lucky enough to get Dr. Price as my psychiatrist.

I know my employment at the phone company did not help with my suicidal ideation. I got to the point where every time I went back to work after a hospitalization, I would end up back in the ER after only working a couple of weeks or days. I probably only physically worked for about four weeks from the beginning of April until the beginning of September when I took a voluntary leave with severance. There is obviously more than my job when it comes to suicidal ideation. I was hardly at work and I still wanted to die. My providers at the hospital thought that my suicidality was situational and if I got a new job I would feel better. I was hoping this was going to be the case but it wasn't. I am truly glad that I no longer work for the phone company, but I still get shaky when I have to talk about it at a job interview. I practically start to cry. I still have nightmares about the job a couple of times a week. Just getting away from the job hasn't gotten my mind off of the torment. I then will fail at my job interview because I got so emotional about the phone company and I want to kill myself again. It has been a brutal couple of months here.

A series of distractions worked to pull me out of my distress over these last few days (October 2018). The pain in my chest has been so severe I think I might be having a heart attack. It is an endless cavity. A pain of hollowness, nothing is able to completely satisfy its appetite. It is very difficult to live with this anguish. I have to keep telling myself that the physical pain is due to emotional pain and it won't last forever. It always feels like it is going to last forever as it takes hours of distractions to ease the pain. Sleeping is the only true escape from it. I know this is why I need to create a life worth living. The monotony of my feelings is exhausting. Tolerating the distress is needed in the short term. However, I cannot live my life as one series of distractions after another. Eventually the dominoes will stop falling and I will need to find something that will have a lasting effect. This is why my psychiatrist tells me that I need to create a life that is interesting enough that I just want to live. A life in which thoughts of suicide come few and far between. A life in which the moments of peace will outweigh the moments of dread. I am working on creating this life. It is difficult to do. I have to keep on trying and find things that do bring me joy. Writing has been a large part in my creation of a life worth living. I just need to find the other pieces to glue my shattered self back together.

Other factors contributing to my suicidal ideation has to do with a deep depression and severe anxiety. I feel like a complete loser as I have not found a job yet. I fear the financial ruin that is going to be inevitable with all of this time without working. I am having a lot of issues with perceived abandonment and rejection right now. I cannot see a future in which I am content. In my psychoscribble that follows this chapter, I do write about a life worth living. I wrote that in August 2018. Now in November, I cannot picture it. It seems as if I am continually making bad decisions as to what Jenga piece to pull out of the stack. The tower is going to crash soon.

I have felt extremely suicidal this whole month of November. I have had to use a lot of distractions to help me get through each painful minute. I am feeling miserable as I am typing this paragraph now, November 15th, 2018. I am picturing my death in my head as I type. I want to get up and go to the store to load up on various over-the-counter drugs and get a bottle of vodka.

Yet, I still sit here and type. I wouldn't say that it was hope that is keeping me tied to my keyboard. I think about my family and what it would do to them. Right now, that is not enough for me. I can picture my last breaths before I sink down into the bathtub to drown. Why do I stay here writing then? It might be the fact that I feel too depressed to go to the store for supplies. Maybe I fear that death won't just be darkness in which nothing exists. I had a nightmare the other night that I died and I had to repeat an even more brutal life than the one I just ended. Maybe I figure that it is not too long before I go to bed. I should be able to handle four more hours, I think. I am also telling myself that I should get up and go to the store. There is quite the battle going on in my mind right now. I am just going to have to tough it out as I have done hundreds of times before. I feel weak right now as my emotions are flooding over. I really am the only person who can keep me from committing suicide. I am going to stop writing for now and distract myself with a comedy. Distract, distract, distract, have to trick the mind.

The following psychoscribble includes three writings Dr. Price asked me to do for him in late August 2018. He wanted me to write a piece of what the future would look like if I did successfully commit suicide. He said I should then write a piece about my future in which everything would remain stagnant and the same thoughts and emotions would remain on the monotony train. The third piece was for me to write about a life worth living. This was a very helpful exercise for me. It was a lot more emotionally difficult to write about my suicide than I thought it would be. I always thought in my mind that everyone would be better off with me dead. I pictured my coworkers throwing a party because I was no longer around. This is what I thought. When I went to write the piece, I found myself looking past my emotion mind and I wrote a fairly honest piece for what I would perceive would happen. Writing this piece brought tears to my eyes. I also thought that writing about my life worth living was just going to be a fantasy world that no human could ever obtain. It was actually a fairly valid reflection as to what I would want my life to look like. The writing where everything stays the same in my future was difficult to write because it is a future I do not want, but I fear I am destined to have. If you decide to tackle this on your own, it is really helpful to write about all three of the futures. A lot of emotions will spill out as you are writing but it might feel cleansing. I know it was cleansing to me. I still go back to read the piece on my death. It has helped me get through several times when I felt suicidal. I would remember the sadness I felt when I was writing about my children. As long as I think about this writing and do not impulsively take a bunch of pills, I have successfully staved off suicide. I cannot say it has worked every time, as my near fatal attempt happened in September 2018. That was a more impulsive act. I was feeling very lonely and never thought to re-read my own work. Minutes felt like hours. The pain got so severe that I impulsively took a bunch of my Thorazine. I did not think about what I was doing until Jason came home. I told him to take me to the ER as I knew I took a fatal overdose of Thorazine (per internet research).

I am also including a one-sided screaming match I had with suicidal ideation the night before I needed to bring Dr. Price my stockpile of medications (September 20th, 2018). I had enough Thorazine and Trazadone to be able to die as long as I did not ask for help and end up in the ER. I was having a brawl in my mind. I did not want to give up the pills as it was my safety blanket. I wanted to make sure I had a way out if I needed it. I also knew that because of my impulsivity that I did need to give up the pills. It was a back-and-forth match that went off and on most of the evening.

Dr. Price asked me to write about my near fatal overdose on Thorazine, he thought the overdose was in relation to some sort of rejection. I had not felt a rejection before this overdose, just loneliness, which I suppose is a form of perceived abandonment. I have included this writing as well.

A couple of friends of mine said I should write about the overdose for my own healing experience. As the piece I wrote for Dr. Price was requested and it had a goal for me to figure out what rejection occurred to lead me to my impulsive act, they said I should write for myself on the experience. It could very well help me when I am highly suicidal, to remember death almost happened. To remind me of what it felt like both the highs and the lows. There are various styles of psychoscribble to show my internal battle.

At this time, I would agree that all of my suicidal thoughts do go back to my Thorazine overdose. I think about how easy it can be to actually die with the proper cocktail of drugs and alcohol and a setting where I am completely cut off from the world. This is both comforting as well as anxiety provoking. The struggle is between the part of me who just wants peace and wants to die versus the part who wants to be a survivor. It is like I am tiptoeing on dental floss trying to not fall into the abyss.

If you are going to take any writing suggestions from this chapter, I would suggest trying out the three writings of a future with suicide, a future in which nothing really changes, and a future of a life worth living. It is very insightful to take a look at your future with three different outcomes. I do believe that the most important piece to write is that of your own suicide. The close second would be about a life worth living, seeing a future that isn't all bleak gives hope. I agree with my friends that writing about one of your near-fatal suicide attempts is helpful to look at during a time that you cannot shake suicidal ideation out of your head. Just reading the piece will put space between making an attempt and maybe the words written will remind you that you are a survivor.

Future with my Death

It is a crisp early morning. Two people walking on the Portland Trails notice something off the trail. Is that a person? They walk over and the smell of piss and shit makes them want to gag. My body is lifeless. My face had been a shade of blue as I had lost my oxygen under my plastic bag and now it is a pale white. They do not need to check my pulse to know that I am dead. Littered around me are several empty pill bottles and an empty fifth of vodka that has tape on it with the words "For suicide use only." They call 911. The police treat it like a crime scene. My body is sent to the morgue and they now have the task of finding out who I was in order to notify the family. The police cannot rule out homicide but all signs point to suicide.

Jason had to wait 24 hours before he could report me missing. However, he had called that morning when I was no where to be found. He explained my mental illness to the dispatcher so a brief report had been made but they said nothing could be official for 24 hours. This brief report helped lead the police to inquiring Jason if I was his wife and he had to go to the morgue to identify the body.

Jason dreaded receiving this call. He burst into tears and started to have a severe anxiety attack. He knew in his heart that the body would be mine. He did not want to pull the kids out of school just yet. He wasn't planning on having them go to the morgue anyway. There was always the slight chance that it was not my body found on the Portland Trails near our house.

Jason crumbled into a heap and started to cry uncontrollably when he saw my lifeless body. It took him over an hour to be able to get the composer to be able to drive back home. He called his mother crying as he has no idea how he is going to tell the children that their mother lost her battle with her mental illness.

The kids could not stop crying. Io was in instant fetal position. I am sure suicide plagued his mind as he was an inconsolable heap on the floor. My step children are at the house and they are crying as well. Neither of them can remember life without me. They had lucked out in not getting an evil step mother.

After the police had interviewed Jason, they did finally determine the cause of death was a suicide. I was the classic case. I have had so many stints in and out of the hospital for suicide that it was determined that I took my own life as I couldn't go on living. My story did not make the news. Even in the small state of Maine, my suicide is not covered. Had it been a homicide I would have made the evening news, but as I was so clearly a pathetic hopeless case my story was never told.

I had always wanted to be cremated. I wanted to be cremated with all of my diaries but they have disappeared. Jason would rather have me thrown into a pit inside a cardboard box. Jason is far too emotional to do what he thinks is best for the environment when it comes to dead bodies. In his state of turmoil, he has me cremated, unfortunately not with my diaries.

My father is beside himself with my death. His aging body has a hard time taking this news. He can barely make it to the half assed funeral that Jason ended up giving me. My father is a fighter. Like his mother he can handle the pain of losing someone to suicide. He was just lucky enough to not also lose people by homicide at the same time.

My mother seems to think my suicide is her fault. She goes into a deep depression and rarely leaves her house. She tries her best to stay in contact with Jason and the kids but has a hard time doing so.

My siblings are all deeply saddened by my death. They immediately reach out to Jason to see if there is anything they could do for him. They all try to make it to my funeral. They end up getting sad of the loss of their sister but they do not dwell on my death.

Jesse is very lost upon hearing of my death. She can at least see that I am no longer in pain. Amy and Stephen are saddened but it is almost like when a celebrity dies. It is something sad but their lives are really not affected by it.

My coworkers do not give a shit about my death and not a single one shows up for my funeral. They are not affected at all. Kirsten, who? Who was she? Oh yeah the crazy fuck.

The kids end up not going to school for a long time. They frequent The Maine Center for Grieving Children. Io is still thinking about taking his own life as the pain is too deep to bare. He has completely shut down. The other kids handle the grief much better but find themselves in frequent spells of crying. How are there this many tears? They could fill a pond with the moisture that has come out of their eyes.

Jason had been correct and he did get the life insurance money. I had been correct and the credit card debt strictly in my name was forgiven. In spite of all of this, Jason still defaults on most of the bills. Although he had fallen out of love with me, he still is torn up about my death. It takes him several months to get caught up on the bills and get back into his normal routine. Luckily he and the kids qualify for Maine Care and food stamps as Jason's high anxiety prevents him from being able to work. Io makes a half hearted attempt at suicide and ends up in Spring Harbor yet again. Titan, Aeson and Dahlia end up returning to school after a lengthy absence. The kids are doing the best they can with the circumstance that was given to them. They continue to try and hang out with friends and laugh when they can. The house is covered under a thick blanket of agony. It is hard for anyone to see the light except in brief moments. Io can only feel pain and can only see the darkness. My death is the hardest on the child who possesses similar qualities as I had. It is funny as this is the child I did not give as much compassion to. I saw him too much as an extension of myself. I hated myself so much I couldn't treat the child who I felt was still attached to me by the umbilical cord with the same kind of kindness I showed to my other children, my step children included. I had been an awful mother. I know Io will eventually see that he is better off without me.

As the first year after my death passes, the family has become a bit more stable. Jason has paid off the credit card debt and the mortgage. He sold the car so he only has one vehicle payment a month. He is receiving some social security benefits. This is what he has been living off of since my death. He ends up meeting a new woman and falls in love with her. She is kind to the kids and stabilization has occurred. I am sure Jason is now happy that he does not have to deal with a crazy wife. The kids are still sad about my passing but can see that their lives are more stable without a crazy mother.

It does take awhile but everyone, even Io, moves on to leading a better life than when I was in it ruining everything. I am at peace and my family is finally at peace as well.

"Living" in the Future Typical 24 Hour Clock

"Ugh, 5:40am, another fucking day." All I have to look forward to today is my coffee, cigarette and morning exercise routine with my pump-me up music. At least this centers me for the hour it takes me to complete these tasks. I wish the sense of being whole would last longer. I thought exercise was supposed to pick you up and relieve stress. I suppose it does that, but the feeling lasts until my shower. No music, just my repetitive thoughts and any feelings of elation are erased from my memory. I might as well have not performed my morning routine as the misery strikes me full force. It feels like eons ago that I felt like a human being.

Out of the shower, I wipe away the fog and look into the mirror. I stare deeply into my own eyes. I do this every morning hoping I will figure out who I am. I, of course, recognize my eyes and my face but they do not seem to belong to me. I know it is me, but there isn't a sense of connection. Who am I? When will I figure this out? It is so odd to have such a disconnect from who you think you might be and the face staring back at you doesn't connect. I have been doing this since I was a small child. One would think I would have figured out how my thoughts relate to myself and my body. I am the person in the mirror. I feel like smashing all of my mirrors so that the broken up image would more closely resemble my idea as to who I might be. I am broken. I am shattered. I am miserable.

I quickly say hi to the kids and Jason. I head out to my fucking dead end customer service job making 13.00 an hour. I get into the car and blast my Nine Inch Nails. I am not sure why I ever expected to do any differently. I am the "retarded sister" of my family. I luckily qualify for food stamps and heating assistance. My life was never supposed to be like this. Well, I should say, I should have handled my money better and gone for a useful degree. My grandfather wasted his time inventing Seconal on me. I never should have gotten the stock in Eli Lily. I just pissed it all away. The only useful thing I did was use some for the down payment on my house. Maybe this is where my disconnect comes from? Maybe I felt like I should have been more intelligent and would be able to do well financially just as my parents had. So, when I look into the mirror I am not a success but a failure… No, that cannot be it. I have felt disconnected for far too long for that to be the case. Holy shit, I just pulled into a parking space at work. How did I get here? I hope I obeyed the laws of traffic.

The seven and a half hour work day goes fairly quickly. I am in constant queue and do not get a chance to think between calls. I get a few pleasant calls. Most of my calls are people who are grumpy. I am feeling grumpy now myself. I internalize this so I do not reflect this back at the customer. I provide excellent customer service and help the customer see a solution to their problem. Damn, I wish I could provide myself with this advice later in the day when I get out. Maybe I should pick up drinking again. At least it was a total escape from my unfulfilling day. Luckily, or unfortunately, I am too stubborn to pick up drinking. However it is the ultimate form of escape. I can run away from my brain for a bit.

I decide not to buy alcohol when I pick up my pack of smokes on my way home from work. I am not looking forward to the evening. I smoke a cigarette before I head into my house. At least smoking helps to calm my nerves.

Jason tells me we received another call from a bill collector today. Perfect, why wouldn't we? I used to have a credit score of 800. Of course I was also the master of using the home equity to keep the bill collectors away in the past. Now, I have no equity to use, so we default on the bills. I, of course, do not help out our situation as I continue to have frequent visits to the ER. I really should apply for free care. My mind is wondering again. I haven't even responded back to Jason yet.

"So, have you made any money this week that we can put into the account to pay this bill? I do not get paid for two more weeks as you pissed away my money."

"You, bitch. You are the one that needed me to be home so you wouldn't kill yourself. I bought things that we need. You should be making more money. You were the one that chose to make so little money."

"Fuck that shit! I cannot fucking help it if I am incompetent and have a mental illness. You could start to fucking work more you goddamned asshole."

"Again, you are the one who doesn't want me working so much. You get fucking bored and start online affairs, remember? You are the one who is always threatening suicide. What else am I supposed to do you manipulative, cunt?"

"FUCK YOU!!! I fucking hate you. I wish I had an online affair. At least that would make me feel wanted. Get out of my fucking sight. I am going to take a bunch of pills and jump off a bridge. Or, I am going to walk to a bar and see if I can get picked up by some drunk asshole who will buy me drinks. If I am lucky, he will be crazy and kill me"

"Don't you fucking leave this house. I'll call the cops."

"Fine, call the cops, I am just going to grab my AirPods and go for a fucking walk. Don't take me so fucking seriously. I want to die but I am going to try to chill with music and a power walk. There is only so much stress I can take. I need some air. You do what you want. I'm fucking out of here."

Jason and I exchange some physical reactions to one another. He is pushing me and getting into my face with his eyes looking evil. I punch his chest.

"Fine! I am not going to kill myself. I am going to come home. Just let me leave so I can use a goddamn fucking coping skill."

I put my ear pods in and stomp out of the house. The walk with my Depeche Mode helps me bring my anger down a notch. God, I fucking suck at using my coping skills before I escalate too quickly. It is just a knee jerk reaction. It's a series of events at work in which I suppress my emotions and then one little comment at home sends me through the roof. It was just a factual statement. A bill collector called. It is both of our faults that we do not bring in enough money to survive. I wonder how much of my yelling at Jason was really me yelling at myself?

My music is interrupted. My phone is ringing. Oh, god, it's my mother. I don't know how long I can keep avoiding her calls. I feel like I am getting somewhere in my brain right now with my emotions. Can I handle pretending to be in a pleasant mood? Can I sound positive and upbeat? I take too long making my decision and the call goes to voicemail. Now I feel the guilt of avoiding my mother. She is a great mother. I do not know why I keep avoiding her except that I feel like I need to be upbeat as she gets so weird when I am depressed. She then goes all into that I probably have Asperger's I was just never diagnosed. Plus she will go into maybe it was because I thought I was bisexual. No, I did not think I was bisexual I am bisexual. God, what kind of a daughter am I? Avoiding my mother because I don't want to talk about possibly having Asperger's and I do not want to pretend to be upbeat.

Now where the fuck was I in my head trying to figure out this fight with Jason? I really had the image in my head of death and that is all I wanted at the moment. Goddamn, I lost my fucking train of thought because my brain is in too many places at once. All I know is when I get home I am going to have to apologize for my behavior. I suppose I should talk about my fears that we might become bankrupt and lose the house. Will it be too difficult to say this? It seems very simple and if I were to write it down on paper it would be logical to state my fears and my thoughts of incompetency as to what led to my outburst.

It is fucking crazy. I have read several books on BPD and on DBT. I have been in the DBT group for almost a year now. Why am I not applying the skills? I do the fucking homework and It's easy to do. I can usually see the logical and rational side behind everything. Every time, I say well no wonder I was super angry at that particular situation or super scared or super elated etc... My emotions fit the given situation. Maybe they are a bit too intense but, that's just part of one of the shards of glass that makes me into the person I might be; or I am? What the fuck is wrong with me? There are people in the DBT group who aren't as intelligent as I am, they get it. I might be the "idiot" Shonle but I do not have an IQ of below 80. So how is that these people with average IQ's are getting the concept far better than I am? I cannot blame it on the fact that I find many of the activities to be highly elementary. I guess I can only blame myself. Perhaps I am fearing what I would be like if I was not crazy? I hate being ordinary. Still, think about this concept rationally, why would I continue to choose to feel the way I do if actually practicing the DBT skills would help me feel better? Either, there isn't any logic to that statement as DBT just doesn't work for me, or there is logic to it and I am a very sick person who wants to remain that way. I mean, hell, when I was a teenager I thought I was pretending to have BPD as it was a crazy I could relate to. No, I guess I self diagnosed. I do not know why my therapist of years refused to believe I had BPD. My mother had not believed it either. It is strange as from stories my mother told me about her mother, I would not be surprised if my grandmother had 5 out of the 9 criterion for BPD. Now this is me diagnosing a dead woman without any training in psychology.

I cannot keep living like this. I am so fucking miserable. When I was working for the phone company, I at least was making decent money and our financial issues were few and far between. Now I am working at a dead end job with no upward mobility. I am making what many teenagers are making. My relationship with Jason is as good as it is ever going to get. Although I cannot fucking stand him sometimes, he is the only one that has stuck with me. I could try to be more connected with the boys, but they are at that age that it has become difficult. God, am I like how my mother was but I am also an alcoholic with BPD? These kids will need some serious therapy when they are older. It is all of my fault. I am dragging myself through each day. I am physically here but that is it. Why did I decide to keep living again? Oh, right a promise I had made, I feel like I am going to have to break that promise soon here. I have been trying to get better for close to two years here and I am the still mess I had been before I got sober and started to work on my mental health.

I get home and see that Jason has left. Okay, cannot apologize now. Maybe I will do it via text. I am going to check in on the kids and eat something before I take my pills and go to sleep. At least in my sleep I do not feel pain. I eat a 200 calorie dinner. I decide I deserve to eat ice cream. At least the ice cream makes me feel better for a bit. Especially if I eat the ice-cream mindfully. I try to center myself with focusing on every lick of the dessert. I am in the moment and let the coffee flavor melt in my mouth. I found something that centers me for a bit. I wish this feeling could last forever. Perhaps it is because I do not care who I am and how my body looks disgusting in this moment. Shit, my mind wandering. Back to the ice cream and then I can let my mind go again. I need to enjoy this moment. If my life is only going to have a few minutes of enjoyment and feeling centered, I need to squeeze out every last drop.

I send a text to Jason apologizing and stating that I am just really stressed about our finances and I shouldn't have taken it out on him. I write that I hope he comes home tonight. I will be asleep before he gets home as I took my evening meds already and want to head to sleep as soon as possible. I text that I wouldn't mind if he slept in the bedroom. He mostly sleeps in the basement so I am sure he will not do this again.

"Ugh, 5:40am, another fucking day." All I have to look forward to today is my coffee, cigarette and morning exercise routine with my pump me up music…

A Future With a Life Worth Living

I wake up moments before my alarm goes off. It is the morning. I love the early mornings. I get to stretch and exercise before the rest of the household needs to get going. It is the perfect me time. I am loving the muscle definition I have. I am not disgusted when I look at myself in the mirror. I can appreciate that my dedication to working out has paid off. I used to see my thighs as fat. I now can see them as strong. I have given up weighing myself as it really should come down to how I look and feel versus the numbers that I have been a slave to for too much of my life.

I greet my children with a smile on my face as I pour myself a morning cup of coffee. I share a brief conversation with all of them seeing what their day will be like. The boys never roll their eyes at me when I ask them questions now. Words of love are exchanged when they leave the house. Last year I would barely even get a goodbye. Half of the time I was unaware that they had already headed out to walk to school. I feel a glow in my chest instead of the pit of pain that had plagued me for years.

Jason enters the room and we embrace and exchange a kiss. We are back to sharing a bedroom now on most nights of the week. Last night he had slept in the basement but he had not wanted to disturb me as he was out late at his evening serving job. Normally he would still be asleep at 8am when he works at his taxable job, but today he was up early to do some under the table painting with his friend. I must say I am pleasantly surprised and elated that he is now taking work seriously and will work upwards of 60 hours a week at times. I would work more but I have found ways to fill my time with other things such as volunteer work.

I sip the last of my coffee and then brush my teeth before I head out to my job. I am a peer support specialist. I am currently working on the Intentional Warm Line and have thought about seeing if I can work in the hospitals instead or as well to add variety to my daily structure. I do have the advantage that I had been duel diagnosis so I have a lot of knowledge and experience

I can share. I love this job. It pays shit but I am actually feeling content. I wish I had gotten into this field earlier.

I know I couldn't get into the field until I took my mental health recovery seriously. I had always listened to the recommendations of my treatment team as to what I needed to do for a successful recovery. I thought the DBT tasks/work were menial at first but then something sunk in. I cannot stop an emotion from happening. I can now control how strongly that emotion takes over. It use to control my whole day, hell my whole life, in actuality. I still feel things very intensely but it is not the same. I used to get stuck on a particular moment and what I did wrong in the situation which would always send me spiraling out of control as the black and white thinking had a strong hold over me. I am not sure why it took me so long to get into a place of balance. I was famous of switching back and forth between rational and emotional mind. I thought I was bringing the two pieces together a lot more than I was. I would think of both sides equally but they were never connected by a bridge. It was two completely different thoughts coexisting at the same time but if they did not communicate with one another, there was no way to be at peace. Writing has definitely helped me with grasping the concept of wise mind. It is the much needed breath to take before an instant reaction. This worked very well when I think of future events. Now it comes naturally and I can resolve the conflict in mind before I react. I do the writing in my mind.

My job goes very smoothly. The Intentional Warm Line is busy but as it is work that I enjoy; I do not mind at all. I like to be busy. I do get a person like myself on the phone everyday. I love it when she tries to push my buttons. Sweetheart, I am the queen of manipulation. She throws it out there that she has BPD. She is wearing the badge proudly, as she should. It is a chaotic condition and I can relate oh too well. A few of them get pissed off at me when I gently call bullshit. Others love the blunt direct approach I have. I am always very respectful of everyone. Luckily I am empathetic and I can read the conversation and know which way to go from there. I sometimes think things would have been different if I had stuck out my psychology major that I had for one semester. There is no point on kicking myself for a decision I had made when I was twenty years old. At least with peer support, my personal mental health background is the key in helping others.

When I get home I quickly prepare myself a salad and a veggie burger. I cannot believe I was calling myself a vegetarian when I used to only eat one vegetable a day. I enjoy adding the vegetables to my diet. It almost feels cleansing.

I chat with the boys and Jason before I head out to facilitate a SMART meeting at Spring Harbor. I sometimes get a lot of eye rolling when I lead the group as it is cognitive behavioral therapy. Hey, I can relate to this and I will throw in a joke or two. At least the patients get off the unit and get snacks. I have this going for me. I just want to spread SMART to as many people s I can. The 12 steps is not the only way to get and stay sober. I am hoping I can start my own SMART group outside of the hospital setting that will not conflict with the other two groups in Portland. We need more SMART. I

am still toying with the idea of starting a Women for Sobriety group as well. I am not sure if I will have the time though. I am incredibly busy with things I enjoy doing.

When I get home Jason and I have a civil conversation about the finances. As I am making far less than I had in the past we are in a bit of financial stress. It is nice that I have finally had the strength to discuss the financial issues with Jason before they become far too overwhelming. We might argue a bit about who is making more money and who is to blame for the stress. At least this is done in a calm manner now instead of in a screaming match where I felt like the only answer would be to kill myself. I had failed every time, and therefore, ended up in the ER so many times. I do luckily get Free Care now at Maine Medical Center so there is one less financial burden. This last year has been a rough one but my ER visits eventually decreased to once a month then every other month and then not at all. I had owed a lot of money before that time and it was forgiven. I suppose that's one nice thing about making a poverty level wage. I at least qualify for free assistance with things. I used to feel guilt if I took advantage of the system as I felt that people like me did not deserve it. The way I see it is I could just be on SSDI and would be fully on the system. I am at lest one step beyond that and I have private insurance. Welfare is out there for people who need it. I never asked to be born with a mental illness and it is just a fact that peer support does not pay at all. I miss being able to go out to eat and to the movies but I prefer feeling good about what I do.

Jason and I watch a show together and then sleep in the same bed. I like that he is in arm's reach. I wish he didn't snore, but it is more comforting to the nights of solitude in which I tend to cave in on myself. I am still doing far better with the times of loneliness than I had in the past. I am never going to be fully better but at least I am 75 percent healthier than I had been. Tomorrow is my day off and I have plans to spend time with Jesse in the morning and Amy in the afternoon. I also planned on working on my book some more. My book will probably not go anywhere but I do not know this if I do not try. I am definitely in a better state of mind where a rejection doesn't crush my soul as it had before.

I am a work in progress. I still haven't quite figured out who the fuck I am. I guess that really doesn't matter as I at least like what I do with my life. I won't lie, I wish I was independently wealthy and didn't have to worry about bills. I also wished I could treat myself with compassion on a daily basis. I am doing my best. The work is fucking hard but it was worth it. Like in Shawshank, I had to crawl through a mile of shit to come out clean on the other side.

My Near Fatal Overdose To Reflect Back On

On my 42 and a half birthday I took a serious overdose of Thorazine. Although I had been planning for my suicide for quite awhile, the act itself was very impulsive. It's just so easy to take a bunch of pills. Once I started, I had a hard time stopping. I bet I would have taken the full 66 pills if Jason hadn't come home when he did. As they had to do things to clear my airway, I am sure I would have died if I hadn't gone to the ER. A few days ago, just after I came to on the 14th, the thought that I could be dead scared me. Now, I am back to wanting to die yet again, and it's only the 17th. I do not remember agreeing to this life. I'm stuck in it and need to live with it.

I woke up on September 12th feeling very despondent. My chest ached with the internal pain. It was as if an earthquake tore apart my insides. The canyon that was formed had an endless pit. Not only was I in pain but it was this intense feeling of emptiness. I tried to do what I could do to feel better. I started out with my normal 40-minute exercise routine. That relieved the pain very temporarily. I was then left in the house all alone.

The loneliness exasperated the pain in my hollowed out chest. I wanted to run away from the pain. The only problem is you cannot run away from pain. Only in death can you get away from it. I had to pull out all of the tools I had. Many of my tools were very dull, and I do not own a sharpener. I was trapped.

I went to my job to collect my personal belongings and to turn in my badge. I thought getting out of the house for a little while in the morning was going to help me get out of my own head. My mind certainly was not thinking clearly. I do not know why I wouldn't have seen the move as emotional. I didn't and I paid the consequences for it. It was just the whole official end that got to me. Here I was not allowed into the building I have been entering for ten years. I had to wait for my manager to come out with my box of stuff. I actually almost cried. This is pure insanity as the job was the bane of my existence. I guess it was just the thoughts, "oh my God; it's official; I am unemployed, no more weekly income; no more health insurance; I'm going to get into so much debt; shit." I did hold it together and I didn't cry. My former manager asked me if I found a new job yet. I told her I had not. She said other people have already landed new jobs. This made me feel like an incompetent loser. I have been searching for a new job for months now and I haven't found anything. How can my coworkers have found something in just a matter of weeks? I was in panic attack mode my entire drive back home. It was difficult to breathe and my mind was racing. A new kind of pain added on top of the empty, lonely pain.

I got home and paced back and forth for a while. I should have gone for a walk outside, but I couldn't bring myself to do it. It seemed too muggy out for me to enjoy it anyway.

I had to keep telling myself that if I could only make it through the next hour and then the hour after that. I did reach out to my friend, Amy. I asked if I could stop by her tattoo shop before I went to my DBT group in the afternoon. I had not gotten a response back from her. Any person thinking with a rational mind would say, well she is at work so she is probably busy. My mind came up with this thought as well. It was just the feeling that generated from not getting a response back was stronger than any amount of rational thinking. I felt like she found out something about me and hated me now. I thought that I just wasn't really her friend. I thought that she was rejecting me. So now the overwhelming sensation I had of wanting to die increased tenfold. I thought about reaching out to Jesse because I just really needed to talk to someone. My rational mind told me not to bother as she has classes on Wednesday. There was no way I could handle two rejections in one day.

I'm back to being all alone. Abandoned in my own house. The house was so quiet. I just wanted to end it all. No one was around to stop me. I kept telling myself I had to get to the DBT group. I am not sure if DBT will work for this borderline patient, but healthcare professionals think it will help. On blind faith I have to go to the group. I need to trust the system. It was just getting to that point of the afternoon as I felt so overwhelmed and my plan to hang out at the tattoo shop with Amy backfired. I tried to meditate to feel better, but I could not concentrate. I basically just wrote about whether or not I should take the Thorazine. Death was my desire. I still pushed myself to keep it together. Eventually enough time had passed and I could drive to McGeachy. I don't mind getting there early as I have a book I read before appointments.

The DBT group did not go over well. The unit is on distress tolerance. I was like, "What the fuck? I am tolerating my distress and I fucking hate it! The pain is so deep. I want a way that I can get rid of the pain and the distress to begin with." I was very quiet during the group and my pain just grew stronger. I had sent another message to Amy right before the group officially ended. I was wondering if I could go over after my group. I was desperate. I get my joy from hanging out with Amy. It is the best kind of stress relief I have right now. She did get back to me right away that time and said she was busy for the rest of the day. I kept thinking that I was in a torture chamber and I do not have a way out. After the group finishes I will be back to being in my room again all alone until Jason gets home.

I shed a few tears on my drive back. I was on autopilot, not knowing how I got from McGeachy to my house. I wanted it all to just end. Luckily Jason got home not to long after I had. I needed the companionship. He had plans to go out that evening to hang out with some friends. I wanted to tell him not to go. I told him how sad I was but he still went anyway. This was the final straw.

I decided to go to my room and take a couple of Thorazine so I could just fall asleep by 7:30pm. I ended up pouring a small handful into my hand. I texted Jason saying I was considering taking pills hoping he could get home right away before I took any more (I did not tell him I had taken any yet). He did say he was leaving shortly. In my mind the suicidal part of me took over. She said you probably took 10 pills, that is a waste of the stock pile. You have wanted to end it all day, just do it. I took more pills; it was so easy. I was going to stop after the second small handful but after a few minutes I had some more. I had 66 pills in the bottle. I knew that around 50 is a lethal dose for a 150 pound man so somewhere around that figure would kill me. I was definitely trying to not take the full bottle. I waited some more time. During this time I thought about the writing I did about my own death and that everyone I am close to would be devastated. I still ended up popping a few more pills after this thought. It was so impulsive. The pull towards death was strong.

As soon as Jason pulled into the driveway, I went to the bathroom to take several more pills. I came out and told him that I needed to go to the ER. This was me thinking about the devastation the kids would feel. After the fact I thought about the writing I had done about my successful suicide. I guess I also got a little scared as we counted the remaining pills in the jar it was determined I took 47 pills. Jason drove me to the hospital. The staff got me right into the ER. I don't remember a lot, but Jason said they worked on me until about three in the morning and I had gotten there before nine. I stopped breathing for a while and they had to do different things to get me to breathe again. Had I just went to bed after taking all of the pills I am pretty sure I would have died. Perhaps it would have been a comma, but I would have been in rough shape.

I am no longer going to have a script for Thorazine. Dr. Price wants me to bring in all that I have. I have to bring in all of the stock piled meds. I hate having to do this. I like knowing I can die. Again, it is best for me to give them up. Goddamn life really does suck.

Suicide Beckons Me Again (For Dr. Price)

It started out like a dream. Was it a nightmare? I cannot remember. The dense fog had lifted all around and yet it clung to me, hugging me. Was I invisible? I felt invisible, better to be invisible than to be noticed and gawked at. I had just gotten out of Maine Med. I was at the ending of my son's soccer game. My, Aeson, such a sweet kid and great team player. I watched him play and my heart slowly broke as I knew I wouldn't be able to go home with him. I must be an awful person. I cannot help my mental illness. I do not know why it has to keep me from my children.

I ended up going to the SMART meeting at PRCC before I drove over to my mother-in-law's. The SMART meeting was good. There were not many people and a few new people. I confessed I had just gotten out of Maine Med after an intentional overdose. At this moment in time I felt relieved that I had asked to be brought to Maine Med. I felt centered at this meeting. I was contributing to the group in many ways. One of the brief sprinkles of joy that I have to look forward to. I have to take each sprinkle as it comes. I am starving and know that I will never get the full cupcake with frosting and sprinkles. I have to accept what little I can get. Yes, I realize I am slowly starving to death.

Once at Ann's (my mother-in-law), I tried to not isolate right away. I hung out in the living room. Of course television is the focal point. My brother-in-law, Jerome, lives for television and movies. I wish I could be that simple. No, I have to be a goddamn antique watch that if not taken care of will fail at indicating the time; so many internal complexities. I still felt all alone in the room as the fog still hugged me. I was going through the motions of being a polite house guest. I think I fooled them. I can be very convincing if I try. I knew I was only deceiving myself. Am I already back to thinking suicidal thoughts? In the hospital I was scared by my suicide attempt. It was so easy to just take a bunch of pills. Now I know what my limitations are for an overdose. I just need time to be on my side.

Sunday was a bit easier to stay out of my room as I could watch football on the large screen. I do not have cable and these are my first games of the season. The large screen TV sucked me in. Maybe I could live for television after all? No, not me. I get bored way too quickly. It was a nice distracting Sunday. I only had slight thoughts of suicide when I was applying for SSDI, the other major project of the day. At this time, I was still under the delusion I had created in my head at Maine Med that Jason would get a job that pays well and I could go back to school. I love school. Even when I have a ton of homework, I do not get too stressed. I set deadlines for myself before the due date so I know I will always be prepared.

Monday I woke up feeling sad. I had thought of several things to do to keep me distracted. I had over estimated the time for many of the activities such as dropping off the letter and heading home to exercise and shower. Jason had told me last week that DHHS was going to get ahold of me today. I thought a meeting would happen. That was an hour planned all for naught. I did not hear from DHHS at all. By early afternoon when I was alone in the house, I started to count the stockpile of meds I have. I have enough to do it for real this time and not ask for help. I paged Dr. Price. I hate my brain. I hate how quickly it turns on me to thinking that I would be better off dead. The conversation with Dr. Price definitely helped me. I felt less suicidal and had a few more distraction ideas. Some writing to be involved. I love to write. I prefer when I can be a bit creative with my writing, but I'll take what I can get.

Tuesday was supposed to be a good day. I woke up a little sad but remembered that I had therapy and then ink therapy afterwards and SMART to cap it all off. The therapy was all talk therapy and it went well. I then killed time before going to the tattoo shop by having coffee and reading. I was having a fairly positive morning. I savored the sprinkle of peace that had descended upon me. I slowly sucked on the sugary delight. It vanished fairly quickly, but I could taste it. I went to Amy's tattoo shop. She had created a beautiful butterfly tattoo to add to my half sleeve. I was able to listen and be respectful to Amy's issues she had over her weekend. She was sympathetic to mine. We chatted about random things as well. I had a handful of delicacies at once. My mind was completely distracted. I did not think of my pain. My internal pain was gone as well. Before I knew it, four hours had passed us by and I had my two flowers filled in and a new butterfly. It looked amazing. My forearm is going to look like a garden once it is finished. I felt whole. I did eat the confections a little too quickly though. Starving can do that to a person. I should have separated them out and sucked on each morsel.

My drive back to Ann's was a relaxing one. I only had a short amount of time before I needed to leave for SMART. At this moment, the gloom started to take over. What? Already? I was having a great time just an hour prior. I still decided I needed to go to SMART. I guess SMART was a bad idea. The meeting dragged me down rather than lifting me up like it usually does. It was the talk that after a year of sobriety Jim had never met someone who didn't say they were happier now that they are sober. I was like I have about ten months and my life is far more miserable than it had been! I lucked out and did not have any major consequences due to my addiction. My biggest two reasons for quitting was A. I was told to get sober to make me feel better per my Spring Harbor stay; B. I felt I was being highly neglectful to my family. Now I am still very neglectful to my family as all I do is isolate. My mental illness was better when I could numb out the intense internal pain my emotions caused. I will agree that drinking did not help with my depression, but it was more beneficial to me than it caused harm. I said point blank my life would be better if I was drinking again, but I am too damn stubborn to do so. I was challenged with a look at this moment. I was like, yeah, we will see if something magically happens in the next two months to make me feel like I am glad I quit drinking. I said if I am alive in two months that is.

I felt like a failure. The previous confections I had earlier in the day were ripped right out of me. I had more sugar than I should have and now I need to give it all back. I am supposed to be feeling better by now and I am feeling worse. What the fuck is wrong with me that I cannot be like other addicts and get better? Some addicts have quit on their own with support from meetings and friends and family. Here I am having had five days at St. Mary's followed by thirty days at Crossroads. I was given a lot of tools to use at the time. The tools worked well for avoiding letting the craving take me over. The meetings helped as well. I was struggling with staying sober especially when I would feel lonely or in despair, but I used distractions and determination. I felt empowered every time I did not give into a drink. As the cravings got weaker, my mental illness issues became stronger. My distraction techniques were no longer working on my emptiness. It was a constant pain I just barely tolerated day in and day out. By April, I was ready to end it all. This was the beginning of my downward spiral. I have spun down so quickly it doesn't seem like there is a way I can untangle the mess and spin back up. I am the yo-yo that is on the end of its string spinning frantically one way and then the other, impossible to try and snap it back up.

I got back to Ann's and took my meds and was asleep by 9pm. I was listening to thundershower sounds to try and drain out my thoughts. At 1am when I first woke up, the rain sounds did not lull me back to sleep. My mind was racing. Oh my God, Jason will never get a job that will pay well enough for me to go back to school. My future will just be a series of distractions as I probably jump from one miserable customer service job to another. Our debt is going to sky rocket at this time because between Jason and myself we will only be making 45,000 dollars a year. Reality slapped me hard in the face. How much longer should I continue on like this? If my future reality is going to be much worse than my current reality, why bother getting a new job just to be miserable. Why not take the pills I have now? Eventually, I did fall asleep out of sheer exhaustion. I woke up an hour later feeling miserable. I hate waking up in pain already.

Wednesday, Wednesday, Wednesday, you will be the death of me. I was in pain and only wanted to sleep all day. My only plan was to go to the DBT group, which I still feel is not very helpful.

I was hoping that I would hear from DHHS. I put a call in first thing in the morning to the worker explaining where I was and I went home to shower when the house was empty. I asked if I could be at the house other times. I left my phone number and expected a call back. What a stupid thing for me to expect. I listened to music and journaled. It was stuck in my head that I have the means to kill myself, so when should I do it today? I even upped the anti and bought vodka to be a part of my death cocktail. I was trying my best to make it to the DBT group. I ended up spending time with Amy. We just sat her shop drawing and listening to music. It is nice to have a friend you can just sit with and not have to say anything. I was out of my monkey mind at this time. I was not given a treat at this time because I only felt distraction not any joy. I walked over to the DBT group. I almost walked out in the beginning as it seems like I am a completely backwards kind of person so the treatment can't work for me. The assignment was about prompting event and then the immediate thoughts you have about the event which are supposedly negative and then you need to replace thoughts with realistic positive thoughts.

Here is me:

Event: not receiving a returned text message promptly, like 15 minutes or so.

Feeling: rejected, the pain strikes me in my chest immediately.

My first thought: Oh, the person is probably working and can't return the message, or maybe they are driving (SEE? I think rationally at first, but the emotion has already gotten ahold of me). More time passes so now emotional thoughts start to fit with my feeling: Did I do something to piss them off? Are they realizing I am crazy and are slowly pushing me away? Did they not really like me in the first place and were just trying to be nice? I can then go right back to the rational thoughts. I do this to try and calm myself down. It never works because I call myself stupid as

I wouldn't be feeling rejected like this if there wasn't some sort of reality behind it. Plus, never trust crazy.

So yeah, I was a bitch during the DBT group. I was upset that we are just supposed to accept reality for what it is and be happy in our misery because we might get a gram of sugar to eat during the week. I called bullshit on this. I left the group feeling angry, desperately lonely and sad. The whole ride home, well to Ann's, I thought, where could I drive to that I can consume my three bottles of death? I decided that I was going to try one more thing first. I paged Dr. Price. The suggestion to write this piece which has distracted me for a bit. I am thinking there was a slow build up to today's behavior of buying the vodka and just thinking about dying and not telling anyone this time so I wouldn't be saved. I still don't believe there was a rejection. The closest thing was feeling like a failure because I am more miserable being sober than being a drunk. I definitely felt very lonely so there was an imagined abandonment fear. Rejection is often the block that causes my tower to crash, but this time it was not. Here we are, with the chain of events. I am feeling too tired to kill myself now as it would be nice to do it outside of this house. So that's what I have to deal with. I hope tomorrow won't be worse. If it is, I don't know if my impulsivity would get the best of me or not.

9/20/18 5:28pm
FUCK YOU SUICIDAL IDEATION! GET OUT OF MY HEAD!
I MADE A PROMISE! REMEMBER HOW SAD IT WAS TO
WRITE ABOUT OUR DEATH? WHAT IT WOULD DO
TO THE FAMILY? FUCK YOU. WHAT DO YOU MEAN?
YOU ARE PART OF ME! YOU ARE NOT YOUR OWN
PERSON! SHIT TAUNTING ME WITH IMAGES. I FUCKING
KNOW THIS LIFE SUCKS! I KNOW I WANT OUT! FUCK!
I KNOW THIS DISTRACTION THING BITES. GET OUT
OF MY HEAD! HA! I'M GOING TO SEE AMY.

6:35P
FUCK YOU FOR BEING RIGHT! YES, THE DEEP EMPTY
IS BACK. WE ARE AT A STANDOFF. WHO WILL WIN? I
am growing weaker. Shit. I'm going to eat now. I'm not hungry.
Please go away. Fuck! YOU ARE TAUNTING ME! I DON'T
HAVE THE VODKA ANYMORE. I CAN'T GET DRUNK.
YES, I COULD GO TO THE STORE. FUCK YOU!

7:08P
YOU AREN'T GOING AWAY ARE YOU? FUCK, EVEN
WITH MY DISTRACTIONS YOU ARE STILL HERE.
THIS IS ABOUT NEEDING TO GIVE UP THE STOCK
PILE OF PILLS, ISN'T IT? I KNEW IT. I SHOULD HAVE
BROUGHT THEM IN EARLIER THIS WEEK. I'M GOING
TO DRAW A PICTURE AND SEE WHAT HAPPENS. SHIT!
I KNOW I WILL NEVER HAVE A LIFE WORTH LIVING. I
JUST HAVE TO ACCEPT THAT. GOD, THE PAIN IN MY
CHEST FUCKING HURTS! YOU ARE LIKE DEALING
WITH A CRAVING. I CAN… ERRR. STOP IT! I NEED
A CIGARETTE.

7:48P
SHUT UP! I KNOW IF WE GIVE UP OUR PILLS WE LOSE
OUR SURE THING OUT. DON'T YOU KNOW I HAVE
BEEN DREADING IT? YOU MAKE A GOOD ARGUMENT.

BUT PLEASE REMEMBER THE KIDS. WE HAVE A COUPLE OF FRIENDS NOW. PLEASE DON'T MAKE ME. I KNOW YOU WON'T SHUT UP UNTIL I DO TAKE THE PILLS. YES I KNOW THIS IS THE FINAL CHANCE. I MIGHT HAVE TO DRIVE TO THE ER. PLEASE. I'M GETTING MY CREATIVITY BACK. YEAH NOT A GREAT REASON TO LIVE. PER DBT, I AM SUPPOSED TO JUST LIVE WITH THIS PAIN. I KNOW IT SUCKS. AMY LIKES US. DAMN! IT'S 8PM, BITCH! I CAN TAKE MY MEDS AND SLEEP. YOU HAVEN'T ATTACKED ME IN MY SLEEP YET. I KNOW I DON'T WANT TO ACCEPT A WORLD OF MISERY. I WIN. Tomorrow will be emotional handing over the pills to Dr. P. I am just going to watch Sunny on my computer. Please enjoy with me.

CHAPTER SIX

What's Going to Happen? What If...

Anxiety has been an issue I have had to deal with since I was ten. My gut would be in severe pain, and I had no idea where the pain was coming from. My family had recently moved, and I think this caused the onset of anxiety for me. I wasn't sure what was going to happen in this close-knit town. I hate the unknown. It could be the unknown about something positive and I still have extreme fear. I feel so trapped by my negative thoughts and my emotions. It seems like there is no way to get around my feelings. I fear that the worst possible outcome is going to happen, and therefore I chose to run to a quick fix to relieve the pressure and pain. I know that writing has helped me in some moments of anxiety, especially if it is anxiety about something a week or more in the future. It can help me see some clarity as to what the different parts of me are saying. Usually anxiety is paired up with depression or anger or both. I just have so much fear I have a really hard time going out and trying something new. I freeze up at job interviews because I fear that I won't be good at the job. I fear moving on from relationships that might not be the best for me as I do not know what the alternative looks like.

I did mention that I was able to take a few skills away from DBT. I know that using mindfulness skills such as grounding is very helpful to ease my anxiety. They actually help a lot more than quick fixes ever tended to. It's just easier to fall for the quick fix. I also know that tolerating the distress by using distraction after distraction techniques helps a lot too. However, since my anxiety seems like a constant force, there is only so much I can do to keep myself otherwise occupied.

I know I cannot write out every single example of what is causing me anxiety in a psychoscribble format. I'd be writing twenty-four hours a day if I did that. I have to try and play through certain situations through my head. I usually play through the worst case scenario in my mind. Of course this then causes further anxiety, and I am back to looking around for five images in the room to ground me. I am still really trying to work through my anxiety issue at this time. Currently I have started this chapter at the end of November 2018. I know my relapse into drinking again has only made my anxiety worse. I thought that I could handle the drinking better this time, but I was mistaken. I have been a drunken mess for over a week. I am feeling so anxious right at this moment that I fear I will not be able to pull off sobriety today. I really want to be sober again. However, life is really hard, and there are certain things I do not know how to deal with.

Jason has kicked me out of the house yet again as I was extremely suicidal on a night I polished off half a bottle of vodka. I was blackout drunk that evening. I think I ended up taking several Trazadone as I was missing pills the following day. I guess I also tried to slit my throat. I do not remember any of this. High anxiety and depression led me down the suicidal path. Jason had let me move back into the house two days before this incident of mine. He was extremely upset that I could not keep myself together for very long at all. He is very firm this time. Boundaries, what? I cannot feel suicidal at all to move back in. I also cannot isolate as much as I tend to do. After my drunken episode, I am not allowed to drink either. He had let me drink a week prior but that was monitored. I knew that when I got out of the ER the following morning I would need to ask Amy if I could stay at her house again. Being homeless has been extremely anxiety provoking.

Amy let me crash at her place for a lot of the month November. She said I could not stay for very long, but she allowed me to move back in when I got out of the ER. Rents in the area are ridiculously expensive. I don't even know if I could afford a place with roommates, especially as I cannot land a job because of my mental illness issues. So, yes, I am writing this chapter with high anxiety. I know that I need to be sober to have any chance of being back home. I play the worse case scenario in my head and that is me moving into a homeless shelter. I am not sure if I can handle being in a homeless shelter. I suppose I will have to see. I will reach out to a parent to see if I could stay there for a while. I just don't want to be this burden on my mother or father. My father had offered up his spare room to me, but it is over two hours away from Portland where all of my providers are. I knew I had to ask my mom. She had not offered for me to stay with her any of these recent times I have been kicked out of the house. Asking my mother for help is difficult. It would be for the best to move in with my mother as she lives in the next town over and I would have my own room with a private bathroom. She has hot water, which is better than at my mother-in-law's. I could shower everyday unlike in a homeless shelter. I had my anxiety pills, a couple of drinks, and gained the courage to ask my mother for help.

After a sit-down discussion with my mother and stepfather (talk about anxiety provoking), they said I could move in with them. I was grateful that they were going to accept me. I was also nervous about staying there. I was told that I would be asked on a daily basis why I did not have a job. Also I was going to be forced to socialize with them which causes me anxiety. It was not my first choice, but I was grateful it was available to me. As I was nervous about moving in with my mother, I asked Amy if I could stay at her place just a little longer.

Amy, at first, said that she needed to have her own space so she could grow as a newly single person. She did say she wouldn't leave me homeless, so she agreed I could stay with her for a week longer. We have grown quite close, and we snuggle on her couch which is comforting to the both of us. It is a comforting situation, but we are never going to date, we are just friends with benefits. It really is best to put a boundary up as we are just friends and by me not living with her it would put the boundary up. I have to respect that both of us need this space. Although my anxiety is high about moving in with my mother, I know it is the best move for me to take.

I am extremely upset about being abandoned and kicked out of my own home. However, I do not blame Jason for kicking me out yet again. He cannot have me being suicidal around the children. I wish I could just have an off switch button to take my suicidality away. Unfortunately when the anxiety and depression get too strong, I have a hard time not seeing suicide as my only option. I know that the pit I feel in my gut and the pain I have in my chest will not be feelings that I will have forever. I do recognize this. It's hard to not see it as that way in the moment. Especially as the fear and pain linger with me for a long time. It is also difficult because I know the feelings will just keep coming back and coming back. There isn't a way to stop anxiety. I just need to deal with my anxiety in healthier ways. Again, I know writing has helped me in the past. A nice focused type of activity to wrap my head around all of the what if's. I know I should be writing out a skit or something of the like regarding what is causing me the most anxiety right now. It is something I will have to do. I am just feeling too overwhelmed with my suicidal thoughts at this time (late November).

I have three skits regarding anxiety. The first one was written in August 2018 when I was anxious about the buyout/severance pay to get out of my job. With it being a union job, nothing is set in stone as it is always seniority based. This particular piece took me two days to write. The second one was October 2018 when I was anxious about failing job interviews and not knowing if I would ever find a job. The third I wrote in late December 2018 regarding my anxiety of being homeless and jobless. I knew that I wanted to try and work out these situations and writing helps to get me there. I knew the topic and then I had to create a scene and a plot. I never know where my skits are going to go until they are done. I tend to gain insight as I am writing. My emotion mind can be so strong. Actually being able to sit down and listen to my rational mind is helpful. My first skit is three of my emotions personified. The other two show the tug of war battle between emotion and rationalization. I like to write, so my pieces are on the longer side.

You can definitely do something similar that is much shorter. I knew I was writing about anxiety and then the next thing I did was to pick a place and a very basic plot. It might help you to do this too as it puts distance between yourself and the anxiety. If you are not a writer by nature, just write what is going on in your mind about the anxiety you are feeling. I am not talking monkey mind vomit. I am talking about a more focused version. Maybe my pieces will give you an idea.

Scene opens in the woods at night. There are three people in the woods: Anxious Abby, Depressed Dexter and Angry Antonio (Tony). The three of them are coworkers who have been friends since they were hired and in the same training class together at the phone company. They are in a small clearing of the woods. There is no cell reception as they wandered deep into the unknown. The trees are huge, the moon can barely be seen as the overhead canopy is thick. Several constellations are dancing in the sky. Although it isn't pitch black outside, the only true light is from the lighters and cigarettes the group is chain smoking.

Abby: (pacing back and forth, smoking a cigarette) Oh, my God, oh my God! We are never going to get out of here. We need to keep walking. We need to do something. Oh my God. I am having a hard time breathing (stomps out cigarette).

Tony: Stop being so fucking dramatic. It was your fucking idea for us to come here in the first place. Oh, let's walk in the fucking woods to get our minds off the company's decision. Let's come out here with very little water. Let's get stuck out at night without a flashlight. Let's come out here with a carton of cigarettes because that's more important...

Dexter: Tony, shut up. We are on a fault line and yelling will just create an earthquake that will swallow us whole. The ground is very sensitive and you are obnoxiously loud.

Tony: It was a close one but, the winner for drama queen goes to (drum roll) Dexter!

Abby/Dexter: Shut the fuck up!

Tony: We haven't tried yelling at the moon yet. Maybe that will make this situation more tolerable. Hey! You, Moon, why aren't you bright like the sun? Fuck you moon!

Abby: Did that do something for you?

Tony: Yeah, it fucking got my mind off the fact that you fucking led us astray you goddamn, bitch. Of course, I'm the fucking idiot who went along with your plan to do this escape hike. I wanted to go into the office and practice my karate moves on upper management. But you two said, no, that's impractical, you'll get fired, Tony.

Dexter: You don't have the balls to do it anyway, you meat head. And your karate moves are just things you have seen on TV. How's that treating you?

Abby: Oh right, didn't you get your black belt at Salvation Army?

Tony: I'm surrounded by dramatic assholes, great just great. (*walks over and punches a tree and screams*).

Dexter: Speaking of drama… Screaming isn't going to get us out of here. Unless it does cause an earthquake and we get swallowed up whole. But I'm not that lucky. We are out of water and there is no cell phone reception. Just accept the fact that we are lost. We are doomed. We tried to run away and now here we are doomed to fight over who we should eat first. It probably should be me, I'm the fat one.

Abby: What? We are going to be out here that long? I'm a vegetarian. What? No! Wait, what? I'm going to hyperventilate. I feel like I am having a heart attack. I didn't bring more supplies as we were only supposed to kill like 6 hours as we were awaiting the decision. (rapid breathing)

Tony: Dexter, give me back the drama queen crown. We have a new winner. Abby, no one is going to eat anyone. We are going to die of dehydration first (sarcastically) as carrying more than three liters of water would have been too heavy.

Abby: Will you please stop going on about the goddamn water? I made a fucking mistake. Is that ok with you?

Tony: Fine, whatever. I'm really mad at I those bastards at work. Who drafts a plan for a voluntary exit with severance pay and wants you out of the building before it is determined as to who will actually get it? It's asinine. There should have been a day in-between so we could have our answer before we have packed up all of our shit to only have to potentially bring it back in.

Dexter: It's the same company who tells us to lie everyday, what did you expect?

Tony: I was fucking hoping for something to be done correctly. But all of us know that hope is a cunt.

Abby: Don't get me started on that bitch. She is the reason why I feel the way I do so much. She uses her siren song and I feel like maybe the future won't be so terrible. But then, boom, she fucking spits in my face and laughs at me. Fooled you! You don't deserve things to go well for you.

Dexter: Yes, that cunt told me that things would get better someday. Here I am 50 pounds later and barely able to go to work at all this year. I have been on short term disability more this year than I have actually been at work. She is a whore.

Tony: I wish we had something to anti-toast to hope with.

Dexter: We have cigarettes we can all light up at once.

Tony: Fine, let's do this shit.

Everyone lights up a cigarette and they touch the cherries together

Abby/Dexter/Tony: Here's to that cunt, hope. Here, here.

They sit in silence for a while.

Abby: Do you think she might be what we need this time? We are so lost and have no idea how to get out of our own way. I think we have been walking in circles all day long but never able to see the way out. We might need her song to lure us out of here.

Tony: If we have to rely on that bitch, we are fucked harder than a woman getting railed by a horse.

Abby: You are so fucking gross.

Tony: I calls it like I sees it, baby. Want to fuck to kill some time?

Abby: And what, get fucking wood rash? No, fucking thank-you. Plus, I am still technically married to Jason. I'm sure Dexter wouldn't mind if you put it in him.

Dexter: Shut up, Abby. I don't have a crush on Tony.

Abby: I calls it like I sees it. And you were the one who inferred I was insinuating that you think about Tony on long lonesome nights.

Tony and Abby high five each other.

Dexter: Shut up. Who even talks like that? I don't have... You don't know. Whatever, believe what you want. (*grumbles to self*)

Tony: We determined that no fucking is going on tonight. It's best if we just stay put here. I don't know what we should do to kill time. (*sarcastically*) Maybe I will scream and perform karate on the trees. Abby maybe you can pace back and forth and your monkey mind might come up with an idea as to how we can find our way out of here tomorrow. Dexter, hmmm, I guess you can lay on the ground and figure out the quickest way we can kill ourselves.

Dexter: Very funny. I've actually started thinking about it not even ten minutes into our walk. There isn't a cliff to jump off from and we don't have any rope. So yeah, at this point in time I'd love to. But there isn't a means.

Tony: So we are fucking stuck out here and none of us has the proper skills to get us out of here at night. We should shoot the shit to get out of our own heads. I know I won't be able to sleep well out here. So we need to talk as long as possible.

Abby: Okay, fine. I like shooting the shit. So what were you guys planning on doing with the money? I want to take a vacation far, far from here but know I should probably pay off some of my debt. Just kidding, I'll need it to pay my normal bills. Which sucks, I wish I wasn't in so much debt. Having kids drains you dry. You two are so lucky to not have to worry about supporting other people.

Dexter: I was going to buy a Tempur-Pedic bed, if I'm going to be in it all day it might as well be comfortable. Plus liposuction, I need liposuction because, fuck getting up and exercising.

Tony: Shit. I didn't really think about it.

Abby: Maybe you can get real karate lessons?

Dexter and Abby high five.

Tony: Shut up. I'll probably take a bunch of time off before finding my next job and will spend hours at the gym getting buff. Speaking of which, where do you think you will be working if we do end up getting the package? I figure I'll be a car salesman. You don't want to buy this fucking car? Good luck finding a date you limped dicked, pussy.

Abby: You are the biggest asshole I ever met. (*sarcastically*) But no, you should do it, sell the cars. Fucking intimidate the hell out of those poor people. Sounds like a plan that will not only get you fired but land you in jail. I can just see you putting hands on people. I can't believe you haven't been fired from the phone company. You get so fucking worked up all of the time.

Tony: Touché. Here's to the union!

Dexter: I have no idea where I will end up job wise. I'll probably just apply for SSDI. That way I can just lie in bed for the rest of my life. I've gotten used to scraping by on the Short term disability pay at 600.00 take home a week. No man is ever going to want me anyway.

Abby: If you get that liposuction, I am sure you can find a sugar daddy. SSDI pays shit, I looked into it. You will be lucky to clear 22,000 a year on SSDI.

Dexter: See I knew it, I'm too fucking fat to be loved, even the basket case can see that. So, basket case, what do you think you will do for work if we get the money and can leave that hell hole?

Abby: It's so hard to think about. I think about every career out there and what can go wrong with each of them. I know we won't be able to find anything that pays anywhere close to what we make at that prison we call the phone company. Goddamn fucking golden handcuffs. It was nerve wracking to put in for the exit. Cutting through the handcuffs is tough. The money is just so damn good. It's nice to have money to spare after bills are paid. I just wish the company would treat us with some goddamn respect so I wouldn't be out here stuck in the fucking woods anticipating leaving. (*sighs*) I know my future will be bleak. I'll probably jump from one dead end job to the next. I'll be destitute, but life is hard. So I am actually frightened either way. It's a love hate circumstance.

Dexter: Here, here, sister. Life outright sucks. Do you constantly feel a pain in your chest, like your heart is ripped open? You know, like the feeling of heartbreak but you haven't been in a relationship for years so it isn't heartbreak?

Abby: Mine feels like an endless cave, super hollow. The feeling goes from my chest to my gut.

Tony: Hmm. I do get a feeling in my chest but it feels like heat. I really feel it in my arms and legs though. It's like I cannot stop myself from clenching my muscles and squeezing my fists. Goddamnit, I am feeling that way now just thinking about it. Fuck these goddamn fucking woods! FUCK YOU, CONSOLIDATED COMMUNICATIONS!

Dexter: The woods, this darkness, really does seem like it is going to swallow us whole. It would be an end to our pain. We wouldn't have to worry about what to do about the rest of our lives. Sweet, sweet death.

Tony: Abby, toss that crown back over to Dexter. I am not in pain. I like being able to fight at any given moment. There is a certain sense of peace that being energized so easily gives me. I will agree that there is discomfort and not pain. This world is full of idiots and everyday someone does something to really piss me off.

Abby: Totally. I mean, yes, I am in pain but I feel like I have the energy to be able to flee at any moment. I got us stuck out here from my fleeing. You're welcome.

Tony/Dexter: Shut up, bitch. God, you are such a basket case. Jinx. You owe me a coke.

Abby: Hey, we could be out there in the real world hearing that we are stuck with the golden handcuffs and will have to continue to lie to people and use the shitty computer systems and get yelled at all day long. Not to mention, never be trained properly; never having the right tools. Hey, I need help cutting down this tree. So the manager hands you a spoon, here use this. Ah, okay, thanks. That's going to work really well, I appreciate it.

Tony: Or, we could be hearing we are getting a fat lump of cash. Sometimes I'd rather face the unknown head on. Again, that is why I am surprised I agreed to this goddamn hike.

Dexter: You agreed to this goddamn hike because you like staring at Abby's ass.

Abby: You do? That's so sweet of you.

Tony: I don't stare at Abby's ass, I just like to admire it. That's all. Not a lot of women are in good shape anymore. Well, at least in our age range. Mid life sucks.

Abby: Amen to that. I am finding wrinkles on top of my wrinkles now. I think the phone company has just sucked the life right out of us. We are aging at a faster pace than we should be. Stress really takes a toll.

Dexter: If I had a life to begin with, it is totally gone now.

Tony: FUCK THE PHONE COMPANY! CONSOLIDATED CAN SUCK MY BALLS!

Abby: I'll smoke another cigarette to that!

They all light up cigarettes again.

Dexter: What was one of the dumbest things you encountered at the phone company? For me it was this guy looking for new service. I asked him for the address he wanted service at. He was like, how am I suppose to know that, I gave you the town, can't you look it up? I was like no I can't. He then told me to go onto Google Maps and he would stand outside his house and wave so I could get his address.

The three of them burst out into laughter.

Abby: (*wiping tears from her eyes*) I'm going to pee myself. (*deep breath*) It's a good thing I'm too dehydrated to do so. Hmm, the dumbest? Oh shit, that's hard. I can't tell you how many times I questioned in my head, am I being punked? People are so stupid.

Tony: Well the thing that's stupid and really pissed me off was when a manager put me on suspension for not offering internet to a woman who was screaming at me about losing her state sponsored lifeline discount. Are you shitting me? And this was me, Mr. explosive. They never know when I end up punching the wall of my cubical so hard that it falls down. Managers are so stupid. That woman was getting on my nerves and I would have sarcastically said, oh you cannot afford your phone bill now as it is 15.00 dollars higher? Let's make your bill even higher by adding internet with a contract and you will more likely than not end up getting disconnected for non pay and will have to pay the 129.00 ETF. How does that sound to you? Sound good to you, bitch? But really it would have been me calling my manager a bitch. I'm clenching my goddamn fists again just thinking about it.

Abby: Oh shit, my situation involved management too. I had this one customer whose internet went down and it was the summer time, so what, it probably took three weeks to get it fixed. (*sarcastically*) Because our internet is so popular we are just so busy it takes a long time for our techs to meet the customer's needs. It's based on demand not on our incompetence and lack of employees. We are so great.

Dexter/Tony: (*laugh*)

Abby: So, this guy gets me on the phone as a supervisor after his internet was finally fixed. He said he couldn't do his job so he had to commute back and forth to Texas. I said well hopefully they put you up in a hotel. I mean who the fuck uses the word commute for travel between New Hampshire and Texas? I was trying to make light of the situation. It made no sense to me why he even wanted a supervisor at this time. He wasn't looking for money. He just wanted to complain and I was like yeah, unfortunately we are really busy in the summer. I thought in my head, what do you expect when you choose to go through a phone company who has no respect for its customers or employees? You made the decision to go with a shitty company you dick bag. You made your bed, lay in it. I said none of this, of course, just the hotel part.

Dexter: Oh yeah, I remember that. That's when your manager told you, yes you, Abby, of all people, that you needed to step down as a supervisor and get sensitivity training. I inhaled couscous through my nose when you told me that. You are the most empathetic person at the phone company. Management is full of shit.

Abby: Yeah, it was insane. Fucking cunt, head manager, said she could tell I was rude based off the note I wrote. Damn, if the feeling of rudeness could be inferred from what I wrote, why aren't I writing screenplays or novels because I must be a damn good writer.

Tony: Ha. Ha. I tried to stick up for you when that happened. Of course it only fell on deaf ears. You are like the best supervisor in the office. Management is the fucking worst.

Abby: The worst.

Tony: Of course most of our fellow sales grubby co-workers don't make the situation any easier. If I had a nickel for every time a customer called in confused about why a certain product was on their bill, I could have retired years ago. Assholes, we are surrounded by assholes. Abby, you might say I am the biggest asshole you know but I have never sold someone a product that they didn't need. Like seriously, adding internet to an 85 year old woman's account who doesn't own a computer because it would make her bill "cheaper?" Yes, it makes the phone cheaper but add the cost of the internet on top of it and she's now paying ten dollars more. I am an angry jerk but I do believe in ethics. I hope I get the fuck out of there. The bullshit is too much. Abby, you bitch. We could be celebrating now. Or I could be at the gym kicking the shit out of a punching bag taking out my frustration that I am forever a slave to the golden handcuffs. Either way, it would be better than being stuck out here.

Dexter: Shit. What do we do if we are stuck at the phone company? My short term disability will be exhausted soon and I will actually have to go in and be called an asshole every other call. I probably will be found in the parking lot totally comatose after taking hundreds of pills. I cannot afford to just quit without getting the severance money to get me by until I can figure out what the fuck I am even qualified to do with my life.

Abby: I don't want to think about it. I mean, shit, I do need the money that the job provides. I'm basically the only source of income in my family. But sanity is nice to have too. I wasn't always such a basket case. I wonder what it will feel like to go back to not jumping every time someone says my name? I am constantly on the edge at all times now.

Tony: Yeah. I know one of these days I will snap and hit a manager instead of my cubical. I might swear at a customer by accident. I don't know. We are damned if we do and damned if we don't.

Dexter: Back to, life is pain. Hope is a bitch. Nothing matters. I'm too ugly to find a man. I am so incompetent I will never find a new job. I will be wandering around the street collecting aluminum cans out of the trash. Why bother to ever wake up again?

Tony: I don't remember being invited to your pity party. I definitely would not have RSVP'd.

Dexter: You can't see me, but I'm flipping you off.

Tony: Why bother doing that? Just say fuck you, Tony, rot in hell.

Dexter: I've had a long fucking day. I am just trying to find a comfortable spot to lie down. I need my beauty sleep.

Abby: Yes, today has been a long ass, emotional day. I think I'm going to get comfortable myself.

Tony: You two suit yourselves I'm going to do a thousand push ups.

Abby/Dexter: (*laugh hysterically*). By a thousand you mean ten, right? Bump it. (*more giggling and Abby and Dexter try to fist bump but end up hitting each other's chest instead*). Ow.

Tony: You know what, screw you guys. I can do more than ten pushups and you know it. Whatever, I don't have to explain myself to you. (*grunts and then starts to do pushups*)

End scene.

Scene opens. It is daylight and the birds are chirping. Abby, Dexter and Tony are spooning each other in that order.

Tony: (*jumps up*). Shit! What the fuck was that all about?

Abby: (*yawning and slowly sits up*) What the fuck was what about?

Tony: Our fucking three way spooning action?

Dexter: (*smiles as he keeps his eyes closed*) It was magic.

Tony: What the fuck dude? Whatever, this doesn't mean I want to move in with you. I guess it just happened because we were cold. Shit. At least it is the goddamn day. We better get moving.

Abby: (*standing up*) What direction should we go in?

Dexter: Couldn't we just spoon together until we die?

Abby/Tony: NO!

Dexter: (*getting up*) Fine suit yourselves. So for the direction to go in... Do we know where on a map we came in?

Tony: What, we don't have a map. You have become an idiot overnight. The spooning messed with your brain. Again, just because I was holding you all night doesn't mean we are dating.

Dexter: (*rolls eyes*) Oh, my, God. Seriously? I meant like when we headed into the woods did we head north or east or?

Abby: Fuck. I cannot remember. The only thing playing through my mind was are we going to get the money? Are we not going to get it because we don't have enough seniority? Even if I get the money, how can I support my family? Many jobs in Portland do not pay a living wage. Do I even have any skills for a new job? What if Jason refuses to get an actual job? Oh shit. I feel another panic attack coming on. Fuck, I wish I had my meds.

Tony: Well, Abby and I put in for an earned work day time off first thing in the morning as soon as we got to work and took off from there. What time did you meet us in the parking lot to the woods, Dexter?

Dexter: I'd say 9am.

Tony: When we started walking, I remember I was bitching at the sun for blinding me. Shit. What did I say?

Dexter: You said, fuck you, sun, I didn't need to use my right eye anyway.

Tony: Oh snap, so we came into the woods heading north than as the sun was on our right.

Abby: Okay. So let's head south. I do not know how many times we changed our direction as we kinda meandered a lot. But if we are aware of the general direction maybe we will get back to the parking lot. I am hoping we will get cell phone reception soon.

Tony: Don't use that word, Abby. It's like the equivalency of saying Macbeth in a theatre.

Abby: Sorry, I should say what you would say. We better get fucking cell reception soon. Fuck you, you stupid cell towers!

Tony: Perfect, learning from the master.

Abby: Okay let's start walking as quickly as we can heading south. Once the sun gets overhead, we are going to be dying of thirst. And before either of you can fucking say anything, I'm sorry. I'm sorry I thought it would be too damned heavy to carry more water.

They all light up cigarettes as the morning nicotine is much needed before the walk that lies ahead of them. What's five more minutes, anyway? They put out the smokes and head south into a deeply wooded area.

Abby: Walking usually helps to calm me down. I don't know why I seem to be getting more anxious with each step.

Dexter: I am definitely getting more anxious with each step. My heart feels like it's going to explode.

Tony: Your heart feels like it's going to explode because you are a fat ass.

Dexter: Touché.

Abby: No, I mean there is this sense of doom. Like we are going to walking forever and never get out. We are stuck out here just like we've been stuck with the golden handcuffs for years.

Tony: Well, we will eventually get somewhere with cell reception and we can use google maps or some shit just to see where we are exactly. Goddamn it. Have I said how much I hate the fucking woods?

Dexter: I can concur with that. The woods suck. Thanks, Abby.

Abby: Jesus, fuck. I am never going to hear the end of it, am I? We better get the buyout because I will loose my shit if you two keep bringing it up during every smoke break at work. Then the bitches at work will hear a piece of it and the rumor that will float around is that I fucked both of you out in the woods.

Dexter: (*giggles*) Yes, that would probably happen. People believed the rumor about you way back when saying you had sex in the bathroom with that other guy in our training class. Who was it? James, I think.

Abby: Ugh. I have no idea how that rumor spread but it was what defined me the first week on the sales floor. No wonder I never made any female friends there. Catty bitches, all of them. I guess it helped me learn I couldn't trust any of them early on. So fuck them, I never wanted to be invited out to any of their stupid parties anyway.

Tony: Yeah, fuck those hoes. If I were to talk to any of them like I talk to you, I would be up on sexual harassment charges because those bitches do not have a sense of humor unless if they are bringing another bitch down.

Dexter: Damn, I am getting so goddamn hungry. You didn't pack any granola bars or anything did you, Abby?

Abby: I am the worst. So, no.

Tony: I wonder how far we have walked thus far? Are we all sure we are still headed south?

Abby: I think so based on the sun, but we can use the compass on the phone. (*pulls out her phone and uses the compass*) We are headed south west. So maybe head south east instead?

Tony: Why south east? Why not aim for directly south as these woods do not go on forever and one direction will eventually get us out. Fuck!

Dexter: Yeah let's just keep heading in the direction we were going. Yesterday we kept turning around and around. We only got lost.

Abby: Okay, fine. But we will just keep going straight from here.

Dexter: Always forward, never straight.

Tony: That joke is so over used, Dexter. I fucking hate it now.

Dexter: Sorry. I am trying to make the best out of these shitty circumstances. I would much rather be sitting in the dark in my bed room chain smoking cigarettes rather than taking in this fresh air. Fuck it, I am going to have a smoke as we walk, can we take the pace down a little you guys?

They all light up cigarettes and rest for a few minutes.

Tony: Do you guys hear running water?

Abby: No, I don't. But I'm going deaf in my old age. I don't think there was supposed to be water around here. You don't think we are walking further into the woods? Fuck! Shit! I need to get out of here. I would like to see my kids again. Deep breathing exercise is shit compared to my anti anxiety meds. Fuck.

Tony: Well, I hear running water. Over there (*he points to the East*) I think we should head to it. Rivers tend to lead to larger bodies of water. There is a pond not too far from where we came in to park our cars. Plus, I would think it would be a place tourists would like to hike. We might find people.

Dexter: Maybe there will be cell reception near the water then? As there will be more of a clearing?

Abby: Okay, if you guys say so. I just don't remember a river being out in these woods.

They all head east in silence for a while. Running water can clearly be heard at this time. They reach a path near a river that is gurgling.

Tony: Are you shitting me, Abby?

Abby: What?

Tony: There is very clearly a trail here. We could have been walking on a goddamn trail this whole time? You said there wasn't a trail. Your ass is no longer cute. I hate you.

Abby: Sorry, I thought going off road was going to help distract us further.

Dexter: Tony is right, fuck you, Abby, your ass isn't cute.

Abby flips the two guys off.

Tony: So according to my compass we should head this direction on the path. (*he points south*)

Abby: Ok, the trail will definitely lead us somewhere. Some of the trails are really long though. So, here's hoping…I mean fingers crossed, it won't be one of the ten mile trails.

Dexter: God, I wish we could drink out of that river.

Abby: Don't do it.

Dexter: I won't, mom.

They walk in silence for a bit longer all seem to be in deep thought. Abby's phone vibrates in her pocket.

Abby: Oh, shit guys! My phone vibrated. I must have cell reception. (*quickly removes the phone from her pocket and unlocks it*). I have a few text messages. Let me see what they are about. Jason was worried I did not come home, probably because he couldn't go out dancing. And a picture of fellow union stewards getting wasted. Perfect, that really helps my sobriety. Shit. Where is the text about who gets the buyout? God fucking damn it! What is this shit?

Tony: I have reception now, too. I do not have any texts. Let me check out my email. The union actually usually sends out info via email. Right, Abby? (*he scrolls through his phone*). Oh snap, there is an email from CWA local 1400. Dear Antonio you were accepted for the voluntary lay off. We are sorry to see you go and wish you the best in your future endeavors. OH SHIT! Boom ten thousand dollars minus taxes and my week and a half of unused vacation time. AND the 30 thousand lump sum! Woo hoo! (*up to the sky*) I beat you Consolidated! You can suck my hairy balls! I am finally free.

Abby: (*looking up from her phone*). Oh my god! I haven't a job in the world! The golden handcuffs are broken! Woo hoo! Oh, shit. I haven't a job in the world. Oh, fuck, oh fuck (*pacing back and forth, tears form in her eyes*). Oh my god what did I do? Oh shit, oh shit. How am I going to pay bills and after I use up all the severance pay? What am I going to do about health insurance? Oh, fuck. Shit! (*starts to hyperventilate*). Why did I do this to myself? Oh my God! I am so fucking stupid.

Dexter: Don't get your panties all in a bunch. You have wanted out of the job for years. When your manager use to make fun of you about your sales 9 years ago you were ready to walk then. You stuck with the job for your family but I remember you were crying so much about wanting to leave but you couldn't. Abby, look at me.

Abby had sat on the ground and was crying. She looks up at Dexter.

Dexter: You were excited when there finally would be an out with a severance package. You have been actively looking for another job for months now.

Abby: I know but all of the jobs I've been looking at pay so shitty. I was only going to quit if I could find a job making at least 45,000 a year. Fuck me! Oh, shit (*breathing shallow quick breaths*). My kid needs braces on October 1st. What the fuck? I just can't. I need the insurance to go towards the braces. Insurance ends on September 30th. Oh, my God. What did I do? It is done there is no going back now. Maybe Dexter and I can form a suicide pact. I can't even…

Tony: *(interrupting)* Abby, seriously. Pull your shit together. This was the news, dare I say it, you were hoping for. You will have money to get by for a while. The health insurance situation should work itself out. You put in for the 30,000 on the health spending fund, did you not? That will cover COBRA.

Abby: Yeah, I did put in for that but if at least 25 people didn't select it I will get the lump sum of cash that probably won't be taxed properly and likely will end up owing this year on taxes rather than getting money back. (*sobs*). And if it is a lump sum, Jason will piss through it. The information about that was not in email from CWA. I think we need to wait on the stupid company to tell us next week.

Dexter: Abby, you haven't always had a job that paid so well. You have a college degree. You will probably find a job with health insurance by the end of the month. Please calm down. Seriously, tears are contagious. Please, don't think of killing yourself with me. Think about your future where you won't be miserable at work every day.

Abby: (wip*es away her tears and takes in a few deep breaths, slowly standing up*). Dexter, you didn't say if you got it or not? You drew the highest number in our class so there is a chance Tony got the last package.

The three of them continue walking down the path.

Dexter: I got it as well. It is a bitter sweet symphony. I guess yesterday was my last day on short term disability. I feel overwhelmed with the idea of finding a new job too. I just know that I needed to get out of there. It was not helping my depression at all. I am going to have to be very careful with my money and will either get a job or get on disability, or both. Whatever, life ebbs and flows. I do not see a future in front of me, but that doesn't mean it's not going to manifest itself. Death is the only way to stop your future.

Tony: Okay, okay. I get it we are relieved to be out of the place that sucked our living souls out of us. I also get that the unknown is scary. I really have no idea what I am going to do. Maybe I should become a personal trainer. Then I could yell at people but I'll just be saying positive things.

Abby: That sounds like a better job than car salesman, anyway. The three of us hate sales, probably why we have remained close all of these years. I still feel like I'm having a heart attack, I hope we get to the parking lot soon I need my meds desperately and I always stash a few in the car just in case.

They walk around a bend and see a sign with a map on it. They run over to it.

Tony: Shit, yeah. Parking half a mile ahead. We know where we are going now. The end is in sight.

Abby: We pulled it together. I wish we could all work at the same place again. I like being around people who get me. You guys are going to keep in touch right?

Dexter: I defiantly am.

Tony: Yeah, I have a soft spot for basket cases. You will be hearing from me. And by the way, your ass still is cute.

Abby: Well der? It wouldn't un-cute itself over night.

Dexter: Un-cute? What kind of word is that?

Abby: Its mine. I have to get my identity back, in whatever small pieces it will come in. For so long I thought I was just the biggest bitch because of the job. I'm lost now. I have no job. I work, therefore I am. Now what? I don't work therefore… I don't know.

Tony: You are not a bitch. You are a good person who was forced to do bad things. I like spending time with you, Abby. You might not know who you are, but I like you. You will find that this package is truly the best thing for you. Maybe you will gain some clarity in-between jobs here.

Abby: Fingers crossed. I'm going to be in constant panic mode until I do find something new. Shit. I guess I'll have to step up my game on the job search. Thanks, guys, for sticking with me through this whole decent into chaos.

Dexter: Decent? That insinuates we weren't surrounded by chaos in the first place.

Abby: Touché.

Dexter: Of course, getting lost in the woods was chaotic but it did help us separate from just being stuck in our own minds. I say we should do something fun together when we get our severance package?

Tony: What? You want to do something fun? Did you lose your negativity in the woods?

Dexter: I wish.

Abby: Maybe we could go out to eat and then get some tattoos. I must say not having to worry about going to work this next week does bring a huge sense of relief. I won't come home exhausted every night. (*crosses her fingers*) Okay, I can do this. I am a survivor.

Tony: Yeah, we got this shit.

Dexter: We survived working for the devil for ten years, we can survive what the future holds. I just hope I gain my soul back sooner rather than later.

The three of them embrace in a group hug. They decide to jog the rest of the way to the parking lot. Once the get there they salute each other and get into their respective cars.

The scene set up is a versus video game such as Mortal Kombat. The background for this scene is of an office. There are cubicles, computers and desk chairs. On the left side is rational mind "Randi" on the right side is irrational/emotional mind "Irene". They are waiting for the match to begin.

ROUND ONE, FIGHT

Irene: *(runs in for first hit. upper-cut, lower-cut, high kick)* I fucking said we shouldn't interview at all anymore because we are going to fail every time.

Randi: *(blocking and jab to the face)* Every is a strong word.

Irene: *(backing up)* You fucking know it's the goddamn truth, stop being such a baby and face reality *(grapple)*

Randi: *(standing up)* Are you shitting me?

Irene: *(swing kick to the face)* We are fuck ups. We cannot do anything right. *(upper cut, upper cut)*

Randi: *(low rapid kicks)* What did we do so wrong in that last interview, explain that to me?

Irene: *(grabs computer chair and throws it onto Randi's head)* Are you fucking shitting me? Did you fucking clock out or something? We fucking suck. We are a hollow shell. Our brain is gone and its been replaced with Abby Normal's brain.

Randi: (grapple) Ha! You thief, that's from Young Frankenstein. *(two jabs to the face)* We put on a happy face and spoke coherently.

Irene: (*jumps up and cartwheels, kicking Randi in the face twice*) The fake smile was so transparent a toddler could see it was just for show. Again we are empty, worthless, hollow beings.

Randi: (*left and right punches to Irene's gut*) Maybe you are correct on the smile but how about the words that were coming out of our mouth?

Irene: (*throwing a computer at Randi*) Yes, I heard the stupidity coming out of our mouth.

Randi: (*blocking the computer*) By talking about how we helped customers in spite of the rusty tools we were given at Consolidated?

Irene: (*picks up Randi and slams her back onto the floor, a large crack is heard*) That was so fucking pathetic to pretend like we did our job well in-spite of all of the obstacles. It was playing a fucking blame game hiding our incompetence.

Randi: (*standing up, swaying, a few right kicks to the face*) How are we incompetent?

Irene: (*grapple and continuous kicks as Randi is down*) We fail every time we try. We never do anything right. We are complete failures. Anyone with any sort of intelligence can see that and therefore we are fucked in the ass. We are never going to find a job. We need to just end it all as there is no way we could possibly do anything correctly ever again. (*picks Randi off the floor and swings her around several times before releasing her into the cubicles*)

K.O. IRENE WINS

ROUND TWO, FIGHT

Randi: (*quickly moving in to get the first hit, upper cut, upper cut*) Would complete failures be able to fight so well?

Irene: (*grabs Randi's face and slams it on her knee*) Fighting has nothing to do with this. (*kicks with her right leg*) Or are you getting all metaphorical on me? Sweetheart, that's my thing.

Randi: (*swing kicks several times*) I don't know how you think speaking in metaphor is your thing. *(lower cut, lower cut, upper cut)* My metaphors are logical. Your metaphors are emotion based from your feelings.

Irene: (*rapid kicks*) Emotions have nothing to do with thoughts. I think our years of getting blackout drunk has made us borderline mentally retarded.

Randi: (*backs Irene into a cubical and punches repeatedly with both fists*) Emotions and thoughts have a lot to do with one another. You are too pigheaded to see that. You only want to focus on the negative and then our emotions are that of anger or sadness. Then we give into self-pity. Don't you see the correlation?

Irene: (*jumps over Randi to stop getting slammed against the cubical*) We are mentally retarded, how could I see a correlation?(*light jab to Randi's gut*)

Randi: (*swing kicks*) Fuck you. How the fuck are we mentally retarded? You are so fucking dramatic. Everything to the extreme for you.

Irene: (*low kick knocking Randi down*) We would not be failing at every single fucking job interview we go to if we weren't mentally retarded. I mean, fuck, these jobs are low paying customer service jobs that only require a high school diploma. If we do not get the job, that proves that we are extremely stupid and incompetent.

Randi: (*jumps up and cartwheels at Irene both feet hit Irene's nose*) There is no proof of that. It isn't like we are the only people applying for these jobs. I am sure we are up against many of our former co-workers and we know they never had any issues about lying. They probably say that they performed great at Consolidated and never mentioned the system issues and daily struggles.

Irene: (*upper cut*) You, bitch. Now you are rubbing it in that so many of our former coworkers have found jobs already and we haven't landed a job yet. We have even been looking longer than most people as we searched when we were still on short-term disability. We are such losers.

Randi: (*kicks Irene's knee*) It is a fact that many of our former co-workers have found jobs already. It doesn't have anything to do with us and how we are performing on our job search. There is also the fact that our former co-workers have not been on disability. We have been spending a lot of time on trying to get better. If we were working right now, we wouldn't have the time to do all of the reading and writing we have done.

Irene: (*grapple*) Our disability has nothing to do with our stupidity and incompetence.

Randi: (*jumps up, low kick, high kick, upper cut, upper cut*) Our disability leads you to believe that we are stupid and incompetent. You are blinded by black and white thinking. (*grabs computer and drops it on Irene's head*)

Irene: (*staggering trying to hit Randi*) You don't know shit.

Randi: (*swing kicks*) I know all or nothing thinking is unhealthy for us. I know we are smart. I know we can get through this low as we have been through worse. (*pushes swaying Irene to the ground*)

K.O. RANDI WINS

ROUND THREE, FIGHT

Irene: (*runs at Randi and kicks Randi's legs out from under*) How are we smart as we keep failing over and over again? That only proves that we are never going to be good enough or smart enough. We are never going to get past this low.

Randi: (*gets up, several quick punches to Irene's gut*) Did you ever think that there might be a reason why we haven't landed any of these jobs?

Irene: (*several high kicks to Randi's face*) Yeah, nimrod, I have been saying it this whole match. We are too fucking stupid. We will never do anything right ever again.

Randi: (*jumps back, swinging jump kick*) Did we love working customer service?

Irene: (*upper cut*) Don't be an idiot, we hate customer service.

Randi: (*trips Irene*) Exactly, we hate customer service. It feels like we have PTSD from Consolidated. I am sure that thought plays in as we interview.

Irene: (*jumps up, upper-cut, lower-cut*) I don't get your fucking point. We hated it, but it's basically the only skill we have. We cannot make shit at residential care which is our only other skill. We are so pathetic. We made terrible decisions in life and now we need to live with the consequences of never training for something we can make a living at.

Randi: (*grapple*) Yes, we made poor decisions in the past and we have to accept that. We need to think about today and what we have going for us today.

Irene: (*kicks Randi's gut*) We don't have anything going for us today, obviously. We are not working and just focusing on our mental illness. That is such a bullshit thing to do. Only stupid people would be doing that. We will be fucking broke in no time. We are wasting our time as we are failures. We will never get better.

Randi: (*backs Irene into a cubical and quickly kicks Irene's face*) You are the one who keeps stunting our growth. You are thinking about taking our life because things are shitty now so they always will be shitty. That's how you see it.

Irene: (*jumps off cubical and swing kicks Randi from behind*) History repeats itself. We have been miserable for months now. No, scratch that, years now. Nothing seems to be improving and now we are facing the loss of our intelligence. Fucking wake up. We won't amount to anything and we never will.

Randi: (*handstand and wraps her legs around Irene's neck and flips her*) I think we are self-sabotaging at the interviews. Yes, we speak well and try to remain positive. However, some of things we bring up such as needing to be at a group every Wednesday that will basically take up the whole afternoon. That is something interviewers probably keep in the back of their mind as a reason not to hire us. We don't think to not mention the appointments until we are hired and should be protected under ADA. No, we bring it up several times. We are doing this because we don't really want to work in customer service. Especially not for a third of the pay we were getting. Did you ever consider that?

Irene: (*slowly standing up*) No, I haven't. Why would we do that? We need structure and insurance. (*tries to punch Randi's face*)

Randi: (*throwing a chair at Irene*) We want to work at a job we like and feel like we are making a difference at. We do not want to keep doing something that is miserable. If we are going to be alive, we need to live a life that isn't miserable. (*high kick*)

Irene: (*practically falling over*) But we don't deserve that. We won't make enough money. We will be letting the family down. We are too far beyond help. We need to settle for a shitty job and just grin and bear it for as long as we can tolerate it before we drink all the vodka and take all of the sleeping pills.(*swings at Randi, misses and is barely standing*)

FINISH HER

Randi: I refuse to give up. We did not drink all of our brain cells away. We do need to continue to look for work but we can take our time. There is a lot of healing that needs to be done still. We need to expand our search for a job with meaning. We learn quickly. If it comes down to it, we can work residential care in the mean time and continue to search for something that pays better and isn't miserable. We cannot fall into the abyss. We need to re-main strong and give ourselves credit for the work we have done so far. Our passion and our clarity is found through writing. We need to continue down that path. (*breaks computer over Irene's head*)

K.O. RANDI

Randi: Shit, I never do the finishing move correctly. Oh, well. A win is a win.

Scene opens outside. There is a cliff to the right and a cave to the left (barely visible). Rational "Randi" and irrational/emotional "Irene" are back to back in chairs. Their hands are behind their backs and duct taped to chair. They are also duct taped to the chair by their ankles. Both women appear to be passed out.

Irene: (*lifting her head and opens eyes*) What the serious Fuck? RANDI!

Randi: (*jolts her head up quickly*) What? Wait, what? Where the fuck?

Irene: You didn't do this to me?

Randi: No, I thought you did it to me. Are you all tied up too? What the fuck?

Irene: Yeah, I don't like it. Sorry if it feels like this when I do it to you. Where are we? There isn't anything in our brain that looks like this?

Randi: And who the fuck is in charge?

Irene: Oh, shit. We just go offline when we are asleep. Maybe this is a coma.

Randi: I don't remember taking an over dose.

Irene: I don't remember anything. I think I did encourage us to get shit faced. I don't know if that was today though. My mind is jumbled.

Randi: This is not blackout that's for sure. This is something very different. Shit. Maybe you are right we are in a coma. We were blacked out drunk and took whatever pills were laying around. That's all you, Irene. Do you remember downing pills?

Irene: No. I don't remember anything since we got drunk. Did we get drunk? I almost want to say no. Our drunken days have all meshed together. This is not funny. HELP! We are trapped! Help us. We need to get out of here to run the ship.

Randi: Damn it. (*trying to loosen up her wrists from the duct tape*) Who ever you are this isn't funny! Do you think one of your emotions got away from you and kidnapped the two of us?

Irene: (*taking her shoe off*) There is no fucking way. Maybe it's one of yours thinking she is better than you so she trapped us both.

Randi: My students respect me. We have to try and remember what we were doing last. Maybe we can piece it together from there.

Random voice: You finally said something useful. I am not going to tell you why you are here. You have a choice one side will lead to your death, you are only a couple feet away from. The other side, although a mile away, you can escape to the world you know. Choice is yours.

Irene: (*Wriggling back and forth, rocking the chair side to side*) Fuck you, ASSHOLE! I am going to kick the shit out of you once I am out of here. That's a fucking reason to live. To fucking throttle you.

Randi: Hey, Mr. Voice. I know you said you wouldn't tell us why we are here. Are we safe though? Like are we in a coma? I need to figure this out.

Silence

Irene: Well fuck me gently with a chainsaw. (*moving her right foot back and forth against the tape, loosening it a bit*) Randi, have you managed to get anything free yet?

Randi: No, I'm working on my hands now.

Irene: Try to loosen your feet. I took my shoe off and I seem to be making progress. (*the duct tape is now stretched out by a full centimeter*) Hopefully I will have one foot free soon so I can try to scoot around to face you. This is absolutely the worst thing that has ever happened to me.

Randi: The use of hands makes more sense I am going to continue to work on this.

Irene: Fine, suit yourself. I am so fucking angry right now I can hardly see straight. I fucking never remember a male voice like that ever. I want to get the fuck out of here now!

Randi: (*continues to work on loosening hands, not getting far*) I agree, we are fucked. The fucking voice said I said something useful when I was talking about retracing steps for as long as we can remember.

Irene: I'm nervous that he said we have the choice of freedom or death. I think it's up to us as to whether or not we die right now. Our body must be in really rough shape. I will admit, I fucked up. I should have never decided to get drunk that one time in November.

Randi: I know, I told you we would be right back to where we were last year.

Irene: I know you told me that. I just wanted one night to feel good. So we could feel like ourselves. I thought we could at least moderate in the fact that we wouldn't need to drink everyday.

Randi: Well it happened we have had a rough go of things these last several weeks. I should have been stronger. I should have done a cost benefit analysis. I think I was curious about moderation. I mean we have fun the first hour of drinking and if we could just keep it at that.

Irene: We tried, we failed. We seem to fail every time we try.

Randi: We digress. I think the last thing I remember was getting an email from the YMCA that our qualifications were not good enough. You were really sad about it.

Irene: I know I cried for a long time. It seemed like a great job and it didn't pay too poorly. I do remember saying we will never ever get hired ever. We are idiots. (*pulling foot up now that the duct tape has stretched out to half an inch*)

Randi: We are not idiots. Every single provider we have seen over these last several months say a strength of ours is intelligence. It is odd that they can gather intelligence over a brief conversation, but they do. (*still struggling with wrists not making progress*)

Irene: Well we have been in hospital settings. They are probably use to a lot of unintelligent people and in comparison we seem smart (*wiggling foot up and out of duct tape*) FUCK!!!

Randi: What? You are screaming fuck because you really think we are that dumb?

Irene: (*moving foot to turn chair around, her sock is attached to the tape*) No, It hurt a bit to pull my foot through the duct tape. (*moves around until she is facing Randi*)

Randi: No, shit. You got a limb free. I guess you were right to work on ankles. Do you think you could use your toes to help me out?

Irene: (*working on her left ankle now*) I can't believe you are asking for my help. I want to get both feet free than I will help. But for now, mimic me.

Randi: (*wriggles foot back and forth*) Ok. We need to get out of here ASAP as I think we are in trouble. We both need to drive.

Irene: Take your shoe off. It will help when you get your ankle free. I am so freaking stressed and anxious now. I don't even remember what we are supposed to talk about.

Randi: Last things we remember. I also remember that Kelly, the friend we made at the Crossroads IOP died suddenly.

Irene: Right and I was jealous as she got to die and here we are still alive. I really wanted to kill us after the rejection from that job.

Randi: I know but you only took 25 Hydroxyzine with alcohol, we got through that night. Hell, the hospital kicked us out the next morning even after you said we were still very suicidal. So that was just a cry for help, which didn't go as it should have.

Irene: Yep, cause fuck that. Maine Med shouldn't have kicked us out they should have kept us to look for inpatient. I was super suicidal being kicked out. It felt like no one cared. We cried out for help one last time and the cops brought us to Mercy where we were bored to death. Seven days of our life we are never going to get back. I think you were having a hard time as you like to keep our mind stimulated. (*now has tape loosened up to half an inch*)

Randi: (*still working on loosening the tape*) Shit. How did I block that out of my mind? It was traumatic to be stuck in that lousy ED at Mercy. They didn't even have a TV. I think the voice we heard drugged us as well. That happened a good week after not getting the job and hearing about Kelly's death. Well, damn. Let's see what else I remember. I know Amy kicked us out after the Hydroxyzine OD.

Irene: Right. (*pulls left foot free*) Fuck that smarts. But I now have both feet free. To be clearer on how the cops picked us up. I remember we went to a bar after we were kicked out of the ED. We then went to therapy buzzed.

Randi: Right and the therapist said that we should just live with mom as being out in the living room and socializing was not a bad thing. She said it would be a good thing.

Irene: Right. And then I said that it was going to be difficult, she wasn't getting that. So I put on our coat and stormed out of the office saying we were going to go kill ourselves.

Randi: And then I called the therapist back and complained that she didn't check on us after we stormed out. I said we had sleeping pills and vodka. It was obviously a cry for help.

Irene: That's when Jason came and the cops came. And we are right back around to being stuck in ED for seven days and we only ended up at a CSU when we needed Spring Harbor. (using her toes to help Randi get her right foot free)

Randi: Thanks. So what other major things were going on as we were highly suicidal. I guess it was really rough when mom said we could move in with her and suddenly changed her mind as we were at a CSU.

Irene: Yes, that sucked. So I thought that we were going to be both homeless and jobless. We still haven't been denied on our SSDI. As we are waiting for the first denial so we could appeal it and get through the process ASAP as everyone says you don't get SSDI until the third try. So I was upset about that. Felt stuck. Very stuck. Just like we are stuck right now. You know what? Turn your chair around. I think I'll be able to work on your hands with my foot and you at least have one foot free.

Randi: (turns around in chair) Good idea. Right you almost convinced me that we would have to live in the car and try to sell paintings on the side of the road.

Irene: (*working on Randi's wrist with her toes*) Could you also wriggle your hand back and fourth in the opposite direction than I am going in? Cool that should help. Well, at least you are starting to see things my way here. We are seriously fucked. Homeless and jobless. We haven't had access to our laptop in ages so there goes our best coping skill. I mean we are luckily on Maine Care finally so we don't have to worry about all of these hospital and CSU stays. But otherwise we are more fucked than we have ever been. More trapped than ever.

Randi: Oh shit. We are trapped. That fucking voice put us in a metaphor.

Irene: So we are slowly figuring out how to get out of here. So, smarty-pants. How are we going to get out of our mess of having no money and no where to live?

Randi: Well, we need to stay at this new CSU as long as possible. Oh, shit. I'm remembering now. We aren't in bad shape. We are not in a coma. We are at a safe place.

Irene: Oh, right. We were drugged for sure. I just don't know what we are going to afterwards. We are just prolonging the inevitable that we are doomed. (*helps Randi get right wrist free*)

Randi: Damn you are talented with your feet. I can now get my left wrist free with my right hand. I'll help you with your hands once I'm free. I don't know if we are doomed. It would be nice if we could just fucking go back home. You are still too suicidal though.

Irene: I'm surprised you aren't suicidal. What do we have to live for? Things have never been this bad ever and we have tried or wanted to kill ourselves for reasons such as there was construction noises at work and therefore we left wanting to die.

Randi: That noise was irritating. I had such a hard time focusing on speaking with customers. But it was you who said we had to leave and go to the ER as you wanted to die. (*gets left wrist free from chair*) Now you turn around so I could work on your wrists.

Irene: (*turns around*) Thanks. Yes, I have been known to want to die for seemingly little things. But it wasn't a little thing. It's like the last straw from a string of negative events. I am not that freaking tweaked and emotional.

Randi: Are you sure? You are highly emotional. (*almost has Irene's right wrist freed from chair*)

Irene: Shut up. (working along with Randi at freeing wrist) I have been in charge a lot here these last few weeks. I am protecting us from the inevitable. We are going to be absolutely miserable. I am giving us a heads up about it. So when the shit hits the fan when we are out of this CSU, it won't be a huge shock to the system causing a painful heart attack.

Randi: I don't think you understand how this works. We cannot foresee the future. We can speculate but we cannot know for sure. (*frees Irene's right wrist*) You are only making us panic now. I agree. We are in a shitty circumstance. I don't know if Jason will file for a legal separation or not. I do not know how we could afford rent at an apartment and still contribute to paying the mortgages which are in our name. I don't know what kind of job we will get. I don't know how long it will take to find a job. We figured out that we don't want to do customer service again. (*working on Irene's left wrist*)

Irene: (*working on her own left wrist*) So that basically leaves us with no options but minimum wage paying jobs. We lost our Ed Tech certification as we didn't take a class to renew it. I think our case with DHS is now preventing us from working with children in a BHP role. We have not heard back from Woodford's and one of their questions was if there has ever been a case involving children against us. Even with explaining that it was because of a suicide attempt when the kids were at home. We never physically, mentally or verbally abused any children. Such bull shit. Face it, Randi, we are FUCKED! We are not okay. Things are not going to be okay. Maybe we should just jump off the cliff and end it all. I don't know if our dying will kill our human shell or not. If it doesn't, who knows who will be in charge? That asshole voice?

Randi: We are not putting in all of this fucking work on freeing ourselves to just end it all. That is the most idiotic thing I have ever heard. (*gets Irene's wrist free*)

Irene: I just feel like giving up. (*standing up*) I know we worked hard at freeing ourselves. We still have a mile to walk.

Randi: That's nothing We can do it. We do not like others taking over for us. We need to regain control. (*working on freeing left ankle now*) We can figure out the steps we need to take so we won't be homeless.

Irene: I don't see how we won't be homeless. Sober houses are just as expensive as living in a two bedroom with a roommate. We don't have any income. We might be kicked out of our own house for good.

Randi: I am sure we could stay with our mother in law again. It wasn't bad living there. We stayed in our room mostly and wrote. We decided to write our book then. (*frees left ankle*)

Irene: I hate the lack of hot water. I know Jason still loves us but this getting kicked out of the house makes me want to push him away. So I don't want to go home and shower every day. I suppose he finally got a job and I could head to the house when he is at work if I want to play the avoidance game. I can't believe how long it's been since we've seen the kids.

Randi: I know that is rough. Let's get moving.

They start jogging towards the cave.

Irene: I still don't know what this fucking voice was thinking by trapping us. And I don't get the option of freedom or death. I would think that we would have been on the brink of death and it was up to us to choose life or death. You are right we are in a CSU now. So, why? Why the choice? We are probably just sleeping right now. That voice is a fucking asshole. I still want to find him to kick the shit out of him.

Randi: What if he is just a voice and doesn't have a form? Can't kick the shit out of a voice.

Irene: Well I want to give him a piece of my mind. I would unleash anger, frustration and emptiness on him. My minions serve me well.

Randi: So will you agree to go stay at our mother in laws? It would at least temporarily relieve the homeless situation. I know we cannot live there forever. Maybe Jason will agree to take us back as we are doing a different Partial Hospital program for dual diagnosis. We will be in the CSU for over two weeks. Maybe that will be enough.

Irene: I doubt it. I don't think he will take us back until we say that suicide is off the table and mean it. We made that promise to Dr. Price and it worked for a bit, but not for long. I don't think I'll be able to do it. I really hate our life right now. I cannot foresee having a life that is worth living. Especially being broke and probably having to move a distance away to get an affordable apartment and that would make therapy appointments difficult. So we would quit treatment and then we would be right back to being suicidal.

Randi: Again, all speculation. We just need to up the anti on the job search. And yes, probably go with a minimum wage paying job. It will give us structure and some income. It would be enough for an apartment with a couple of roommates. We might even be able to find sober people to live with.

Irene: What no drinking to get us through this incredibly rough time?

Randi: No drinking. We have already gone a few weeks without it. We have being sober for a length of time for us. We are no longer having the daily cravings. I think we are back to mindset we had after being a few months sober.

Irene: Says you! I desperately need a drink. You are lucky as you don't feel the pain as deeply as I do.

Randi: You don't need a drink. You just want a drink.

Irene: I need something to numb out all of this pain. I know our future is bleak. I cannot fathom how else we are going to prevent suicide unless we drink. I still don't get why people want us to live. That bullshit we heard a year ago that people are usually happy that they didn't die a year after the fact. We are over a year after we started dreaming of suicide every day and we aren't any further.

Randi: At least I have been asking for help. I agree though. We are supposed to have been happy a year after we were sober and we aren't. Everyone is different. Besides we are still suicidal so we really haven't had that year to be happy that we haven't died. I guess maybe we will be happier this coming September which is a year after our near fatal overdose.

Irene: This whole thing is bullshit. We are supposed to be better by now. Yet our situation is just getting worse. I just want to drive down south and live out of the car from there. I cannot see how we are ever going to get out of this current mess.

Randi: We need to work together and take everything we can out of the treatment that is provided to us.

Irene: It feels like we have been jogging forever. When are we going to get to that damn cave? This is such bullshit. I feel like I'm running to a lost cause.

Randi: The voice said that the cave will free us. As there isn't anymore help right now other than that voice we have to try and see if it will work. We do not have any other options as we have no idea as to where we are.

Irene: I know, fine. This jog is making my head spin. All I can think about is that we are broke. We will not get home anytime soon. We might get legally separated and therefore will probably lose our Maine Care as they don't seem to provide it easily to single adults. Without insurance, we are fucked. Without a place to live permanently, we are fucked. Without income, we are fucked. We should have just jumped off of the cliff. I was stupid to say we should live just so I could kick the ass of the unknown voice. We can always turn around and do it. Why bother living such a miserable life?

Randi: We don't know if it is all going to be miserable. We have that book we are working on that will helpfully help other people.

Irene: The book will never get published. We don't have the money to do it and the book itself probably won't make any money at all as we want it to be affordable to people. So let's just go back and end it all.

Randi: The cave is right there. We have to go and check it out. If it is a trap, than we will have to think of another plan.

Irene: Fine.

Randi: Okay, then. Let's check it out.

They walk into the cave. There is one torch. Randi grabs it. They walk into the cave.

Randi: At least a torch was provided to us. It's nice to not be completely in the dark.

Irene: That's true. We need to figure our way out of here as quickly as possible. I hope this isn't a cave with many paths out. That would just be our luck.

Randi: Wait. There is something written on this wall. It says that we got SSDI.

Irene: Bullshit. No one ever gets it their first try I think especially for mental illness.

Randi: Well it says we got it. Unless that voice is fucking with us. We need to believe it is true. That helps with one of our major issues right now. I think it was supposed to be an okay amount as we were able to work for all of those years as a functioning alcoholic.

Irene: Well, fuck. That would be great. If it is a lie, I am definitely going to track down the voice and kill him. I don't fucking care at this time. If someone is that mean, he deserves to die.

Randi: Well we will figure it out for sure once we are out of here.

Irene: And there is the fucking fork on the path. Fuck me. Nothing can ever be easy now can it?

Randi: Well maybe there is a clue to see what path to go down. There might be something written. (*looks around with the torch*) Oh, here's something. It says take the path that is most helpful to you.

Irene: What the fuck is that supposed to mean? We might as well have not gotten a clue.

Randi: No, it was a good clue. It is telling us to take the right path. As in the correct path so it's right.

Irene: (*walks to the right behind Randi*) If you say so. I really think this whole thing is futile. We will get back to our drivers seat eventually but will likely find we are still as screwed. Even if the SSDI thing is true, we still have homeless issue as we still need to contribute to the household we were kicked out of. That will take all of our money as we want the kids to have a comfortable life.

Randi: Well, we need to take each thing as it comes. It's hard to figure out what we will need to do to live a life that is worth living.

Irene: I have given up on that. I do not foresee it happening, ever.

Randi: Well we should continue living for the kids in the mean time. We will find something that will make life pleasant. I don't know how much we can work on SSDI, but now maybe we can see about the per diem on the peer support Warm Line.

Irene: I suppose. Oh shit. There is light up ahead. I think we are almost out of this stupid situation.

Randi: Finally. I was just as annoyed as you were about this situation. I'm used to you lightly tying me with rope. That is easy to get out of though. The duct tape was difficult.

Irene: (*stepping out into the light*) Holy shit! We made it out! We are back to the familiar. I almost feel happy right now. I don't though, because I'm still pissed about the situation.

Randi: Let's go drive the ship together. We have no idea what happened while we were gone and who knows how long we were gone for as we were drugged. If the SSDI thing is true we probably were gone for at least a day. I have no idea how we were able to function without someone stealing the ship but it happened and it might not be pretty.

They teleport to the steering wheels.

Randi: I do not see any harm done and it is fucking true. We got the SSDI on our first try. That's incredible.

Irene: Well shit. Nothing ever seems to go our way. I suppose I can admit that I am sometimes wrong.

Randi: Sometimes?

Irene: Shut up.

End scene.

CHAPTER SEVEN

I Want it, I Want it Now

I definitely have a problem with instant gratification. This is the reason why it is so easy to go for the quick fixes. Some quick fixes last longer than others, but they all wear off eventually and I am back to feeling the deep pain in my chest. The vast hole in my gut keeps begging to be filled. I try to find things to calm down the beasts within me. I know that long-term therapy is the true way to quiet the hunger, but it takes a long time. I want to feel good, and I want to feel good now. This has been a monster standing in my way towards recovery from my mental illness issues. I try not to feed her, hoping this will make her disappear. Of course this doesn't work, why would it? I have found myself locked in the quick-fix jail time and time again.

Logically, I know that quick fixes are only temporary solutions for my problems. I know that I have to get to the root of what is causing my pain. A person doesn't all of a sudden feel like her heart is going to explode for no reason at all. The manifestation of the physical pain I feel in my chest as well as in my gut is my emotions telling me that something is terribly wrong. My problem is that I need gratification as soon as possible, and it is easier to go to a quick fix. It would take too long to get to the heart of the problem. There is a reason why I hurt so badly when it comes to something such as perceived abandonment. I would rather stuff the emotions down than deal with them. Breaking free from the quick fixes is hard to do.

I will admit that quick fixes do have their place. A lot of times when I have an urge to drink I will turn to dark chocolate instead. When the pain is so severe and I feel like it is never going to end unless I kill myself, cutting might ground me enough to ease the pain temporarily. I know quick fixes really shouldn't be used much at all, but sometimes it is the best option to keep myself safe. Sometimes you got to do what you got to do. The problem is always turning to the quick fix for relief. This is putting mask after mask over the problem. The problem only seems to get bigger as it is hiding under the tapestry of temporary solutions.

Alcohol was my favorite quick fix. I was able to numb out my feelings and would often pass out early. It was my best friend. The only problem with it was I couldn't use it all day long as I had to work. I would obsess over alcohol while I was at work and start drinking the moment I walked into the house. It really did the trick for filling my canyon of sorrow that stretched from my chest to my intestines. However, every night I had to consume alcohol to keep my feelings away. I had to drink more and more to hide the emotions as they were obviously growing larger and larger as they were floating in alcohol. I wanted to drown them with booze, but they are floaters and soak up the alcohol enlarging them. It finally got to the point where I wanted to kill myself on a daily basis as the alcohol wasn't doing what it was supposed to do. It was not killing my pain. It was only making my pain grow deeper. This is why I had decided to stop drinking. It was no longer dulling the empty pain; it was making it worse. I am just over a year sober now, and I still remember the times that alcohol covered my despair. I have urges to drink to be able to run away, if only for a moment, from my pain. I do know that if I started to drink again, I would probably be quickly back in the game of training my inner beast into growing stronger. I would probably end up committing suicide in a blackout. I miss this quick fix, but I know it causes greater harm than the couple hours of peace it will grant me. I have not found a coping skill to replace the numbed out feeling alcohol provided me. I know meditating can help me tune out the world, but it is not the same. I suppose the answer is I am not supposed to numb out my feelings. I need to deal with them and cope the best I can.

Update, on November 19th, 2018, I did get drunk. I learned from this slip that I cannot moderate. The quick fix docs not last for long. I was a sobbing mess by the end of the night as I couldn't be happy with being buzzed. I had to get drunk. It was a learning opportunity, and I now know that my favorite quick fix doesn't work very well. Drinking is really fun for an hour, and I feel good about myself during that hour. However, that's all I get. Logically, I know that the benefits of drinking do not outweigh the costs. However, I dove head first into a three-week relapse. I need to listen to my logic. I'm going to do my best to get back to long-term sobriety.

Self-harm is another quick fix I turn to quite often. I do understand that I turn to this as a grounding technique. When I feel the pain and see the blood or the blister that has formed, I take a deep breath and I know that I am in the here and now. For a few moments I have forgotten my obsessive thoughts. I have several grounding skills that I do use on a regular basis. I am not sure why I will still turn to self-harm. I know that there is punishment involved when I do cut or burn myself. Other methods of grounding do not do this. I know I should always at least try to use a skill before I cut. A lot of time the cutting is an impulsive behavior and I know it has worked for me. In the moment it can be very difficult to think rationally. It is easiest to go with a tried and true behavior. I am working on this. Using a cost-benefit analysis for self-harm has helped me. I just need to make a coping skill be my new instant go to. I am working on it. It isn't easy, but I am trying. If it was easy to use positive coping skills from the get-go, I don't think I would have ever had a problem with quick fixes. The things that I've turned to ground myself are things such as holding an ice cube. It does cause a bit of pain and I am in the moment. I will also play the alphabet game. That one is played by picking a topic such as song titles and then you go through each letter of the alphabet trying to come up with a match. I find myself only thinking of this particular activity at the time as it can be hard to come up with things. This method doesn't have any pain involved (I would hope not at least), but it does bring my focus in on one thing. I have occasionally taken a quick cold shower to shock my system into the moment and this is painful. I have these tools and yet I still find myself with my utility knife in hand. I sometimes don't even remember grabbing the utility knife. This is how engrained self-harm is for me. Now it is a matter of re-training my brain to go for the longer and more difficult coping skills. I am getting there. Practice is a key. I just forget to practice when I am not in a crisis mode. This is probably why I find it difficult. I am working on it, and I wish I was perfect but I am not.

Food has also been a quick fix I have often turned to. Early on it was the denial of food and the pain of hunger that helped me. I thought my empty hole would go away if I starved it. Fight empty with empty. Unfortunately it did not work. The obsession I had over counting calories and exercising helped ease the pain. Again, I was just hiding from the pain and not facing up to it. I have recently been trying to fill my void with lots of candy. I know this is not healthy for me as sometimes I will have a whole meal of only sweets. Sugar does help the pain of the emptiness. It only works for a couple of minutes, however. My body dysmorphia is going crazy right now with my new abuse of overeating. I have gained weight; that is the truth. I feel like I am one hundred and eighty pounds. I feel like people will call me fat. Of course this isn't happening. I am still slightly under the ideal weight for my height. I still feel like a gross pig though. I am really struggling with the sugar quick fix. I know I can go back to not eating sweets at all and then it would be under control. However, I like sweets. A good dessert actually makes me feel happy. What I am trying to do now is to mindfully eat my dessert. Taking my time and noticing every flavor, texture and smell at least slows me down before I end up becoming a glutton. This is the only positive coping skill I have found thus far to help with the compulsive overeating. I just have to remember to keep doing it. I can have my cake, a slice only, and savor it too.

Heck, I've even turned to social media looking for a quick fix. I will create a meme or a somewhat humorous post. If I only get ten likes on my meme or comment, I see it as a failure. My quick fix need to be liked was not filled. I then will create more and more memes to see if I can get more likes on that. I know it is kind of ludicrous to place value on myself with how many likes I get on social media. If I do get a lot of likes, then I will ride the high for a couple of hours. This is why I use this quick fix. It is not a harmful quick fix. However, I can start to become obsessed over finding the next best meme. I suppose it could be harmful if people tell me that my meme was stupid. I guess I have lucked out in that department thus far. I know I should take a few steps back and not focus on my likes as a measurement as to how my day will be. I know I should probably stop posting memes altogether. I just love the high from the memes that are well received. I guess I need to refocus on my need for instant validation. In my mind, I am okay if my creations are received well, and I am a stupid bore if they are not. I just need to change the way I look at things. That's all this has really come down to. Maybe the next time I create a meme I will go on a twenty-four-hour hiatus away from social media and get away from the quick validation fix need I have.

Another quick fix for me revolves around someone liking me. I know this is a horrible quick fix to use as I am married. However, I keep turning to it over and over again. I have the feeling it is a lot like having a sexual addiction, but I just don't have sex with these people. I love it when someone new tells me I am smart or beautiful. It is such a high for me. The high usually only lasts for a few weeks. I then end up breaking someone's heart because I led them to believe that I might drop Jason to be with them. This is not a quick fix I am proud of at all. I don't even know why I still turn to it. I have some sort of compulsion that can only be fed by my over the top flirting. I am lying to these poor men and women about my intentions, and I am hurting my marriage at the same time. I just need to be liked. I know it is at others expense. This is a quick fix that I have yet to find a coping skill to replace it with. I unfortunately do not feel the high of love when I am intimate with Jason. I love him dearly, but the love has grown stale. I wish I could replace making out with other people to making love to him and feel the same way. I hope I find a suitable replacement for this quick fix. I am not sure if I ever will, until I can start being compassionate to myself. I need to provide my own validation. I need to accept myself and believe that Jason is telling me the truth when he says I am intelligent and hot.

I see my suicidal ideation as being a quick fix as well. I spend hours researching how to kill myself. I also picture my death in my mind. I know it is a need for finding peace. If I am dead, then I wouldn't feel the pain I feel. I just desperately want to get away from my painful emotions. I would be able to do that through death. I do gain an eerie sort of calm when I do have the pills and alcohol close by. I can think that this moment sucks so much, if it comes down to it, I have my exit plan feet away. The only way for me to get beyond the suicidal thoughts is through distraction. I like comedy. I like to draw something I find comforting such as the mountains. I also find focusing on writing helps a lot. It is so hard to get away from compulsive thoughts. I can silence them for a little while, but they will start screaming at some point in time. I have not found a long-term coping skill for suicidal ideation. I guess tolerating the pain and engaging myself in a different activities is going to be the closest I get to replacing this quick fix. I know that life is more than just using coping skill after coping skill. Or for that matter, quick fix after quick fix. Coping skills will help me get through certain emotions. I need to write to find the truth and work on the emotion that is causing me pain in the first place. The more I can examine my emotions and the parts of me who are constantly fighting to be in control, the easier it will be for me to just be. I need to accept my life for what it is. I need to stop trying to hide my pain. I need to face my pain. I need to see that the easiest path can be the most dangerous. I am still working on this and using psychoscribble helps me.

My psychoscribble piece has the two opposing sides of myself. I wrote this November 20th, 2018. The side who wants and thinks she can get better versus the side who would rather have instant gratification. I wrote out a scene to express this. I have a setting to my skit, but this is not necessary. I like to have at least some sort of setting and at least a weak plot. For me personally, when I write with an idea in my mind, it is actually easier to write in a free flowing status which will eventually come around to see the best solution. I do not know how any of my psychoscribble pieces will end until I write them.

The scene opens with two women in a store. It is a large big box store that has anything and everything. One woman is coping skills, Connie. The other woman is quick-fix Anita.

Connie: (*walking down an aisle with Anita*) We only came here for paints and pallets, remember that.

Anita: Oh come on, this store has everything. I know I can find some quality products here.

Connie: What are you talking about? We said we would paint today to get our mind off of suicide.

Anita: I know, but I don't want to paint. I want to buy a bunch of candy, a utility knife, some alcohol and sleeping pills.

Connie: You are not going to buy any of those things.

Anita: I want to.

Connie: Yes you want to, you don't need to.

Anita: You aren't any fun. I'm in so much physical pain right now. I don't see how painting would help.

Connie: It's a good distraction.

Anita: But it won't kill the pain I am feeling right now.

Connie: No it won't kill the pain, but it will get our minds off of the pain for a little while.

Anita: I suppose. I just feel like such a loser not being able to find a job. I hate that we are stuck in this painful life. I just need something that is going to make the pain go away. (*grabs a package of Peanut M&M's and York Peppermint patties*).

Connie: Come on. We are getting fat from that. (grabs the candy and puts it back on the shelf)

Anita: Screw that shit. I am feeling empty inside it goes hand in hand with the pain. I need it.

Connie: (*walks ahead of Anita*) You want it. It will only fill the hole for the tiniest amount of time.

Anita: (*shoveling handfuls of Peanut M&M's in her mouth, between handfuls*) I am going to do what makes me feel good.

Connie: (*turning around*). Hey! What are you doing? We are getting so fat, you need to stop.

Anita: (*still inhaling the chocolate*) I am not going to stop. I feel a little better right now.

Connie: Fine. I wish you would take time to enjoy it at least rather than looking like a fucking pig at a trough.

Anita: (*flips off Connie*) Shut up. I'll stop. I just feel sick now. (walks the opposite direction)

Connie: Where are you going?

Anita: It doesn't take the two of us to pick out paint. I'm going to look around. Find me after you get the stuff.

Connie: I can't trust you. You just ate a bunch of candy.

Anita: I can handle myself.

Connie: Fine, whatever. (*turns opposite direction and starts walking*)

A few minutes later, Anita has wondered off to the hardware department and Connie has picked up the art supplies.

Connie: (*to herself*) Okay, Anita, where did you wander off to? You already had the candy, so now I'm guessing alcohol or utility knives. But who knows, maybe you are looking at video games. (*walks over to the hardware department*)

Anita is sitting on the ground trying to rip open a utility knife from its package

Connie: Jesus, fuck. Are you shitting me?

Anita: (*stands up and looks at Connie*) What?

Connie: What do you mean what?

Anita: I was just looking at the knives.

Connie: You were trying to fucking rip one open and I bet you were going to steal it.

Anita: No I wasn't.

Connie: Bullshit.

Anita: I wasn't going to steal it. I was just going to see how easily the blade can be replaced is all. I would have paid for it.

Connie: I thought we weren't going to cut anymore.

Anita: I will not ruin our tattoos. We have ankles to cut.

Connie: But it only helps for like five fucking seconds.

Anita: That is five less seconds of this fucking empty pain.

Connie: Use your rubber band to smack your wrist instead.

Anita: It doesn't hurt enough to draw away attention from the internal pain and you know that.

Connie: Well do a fucking grounding technique. Go out and smoke a cigarette mindfully. Go through the five senses. Five things you can see; four things you can touch; three things you can hear; two things you can smell and one thing you can taste.

Anita: I tried that. It didn't work. I need the pain to snap me back into reality.

Connie: You could always try other things. I did not sit there with you through all of this treatment to keep turning back to our old habits.

Anita: If you can tell me about a technique that causes pain and brings me into the moment that doesn't involve cutting or burning, I am all ears.

Connie: Put your hands up to your wrists into ice cold water. Hell put your face into ice cold water. We fucking hate the cold and that will both be painful and grounding. Shock to the system.

Anita: Fine I will try it later. I won't buy the goddamn knife. (*runs off*)

Connie: Why are you running? What the fuck? I am so tired of chasing you. Fucking act like an adult. Are you coming back? Shit. (*slowly follows Anita*)

Anita has run to the aisle with alcohol. This store doesn't put locked seals on the drinks. Anita has grabbed a bottle of vodka and is drinking right from the bottle.

Anita: (*to herself*) Oh, fuck. I love you so much. I have missed you so much. Why did I ever let you go from my life? (*drinks more*)

Connie: (*approaching the aisle*) No!

Anita: (*takes a gulp*) What?

Connie: How the fuck did you drink that much in a minute?

Anita: I know, weird right? It's been over a year and I wouldn't have known it was going to go down so easily. It's great. I think we can drink again.

Connie: Give me that bottle.

Anita: No.

Connie: (*wrestling the bottle away getting liquor on herself and the floor*) How did it fucking come to this?

Anita: You just fucking wasted a lot of vodka.

Connie: Goddamn! Yes, I get that life fucking sucks. I fucking get it. We worked so dam fucking hard at sobriety. Why would you do it?

Anita: I wanted it. Alcohol has always been the one thing to make the pain go away.

Connie: Yes, it masks it for a while.

Anita: See you get it.

Connie: Why couldn't we just go home and listen to music and paint?

Anita: I just want the pain to go away for now. Speaking of masking pain, art is just a fucking distraction. It doesn't fucking get rid of the pain. The pain will dull but as soon as we are done it will come right back. I'm so fucking tired of distracting all of the time. I want us to just feel well.

Connie: Well, duh. We do want to feel well but at this fucking moment in time we have to fucking tolerate the distress and do what we can to survive.

Anita: (*sadly*) I don't know why we should keep on going? We are fucking miserable. We might as well drink. At least we can forget about the pain in our black outs.

Connie: We have kids. We should keep on for them.

Anita: (*slurring*) We need to live for ourselves. If life is just going to be this miserable, we need to do things that feel good. We need to have pleasure.

Connie: Yes, we need to have pleasure. Alcohol isn't the answer though. You are already slurring and I do not know how the fuck we are going to be able to drive home?

Anita: I got it. I can totally drive.

Connie: Fuck. Why? Why, did you drink?

Anita: I fucking want to have this pain go away. It has always been the best solution.

Connie: It only feels like the best solution. How are you going to feel if we get an OUI? How are we going to feel tomorrow? I do not fucking miss the daily hangovers.

Anita: I hate the hangovers too. Drinking will get rid of the hangovers.

Connie: Please. We cannot go back to drinking again.

Anita: Well, what coping skill have we found to completely numb out?

Connie: We haven't found one.

Anita: See, we haven't found one. We need alcohol back in our lives. (*stumbling*)

Connie: I really don't think there is a skill to completely numb out.

Anita: So we should drink. We didn't binge eat or really hurt ourselves when we were drinking.

Connie: I know. We worked so fucking hard though. There are things that are kind of close to numbing out such as playing a video game.

Anita: A video game is a great distraction, I will give you that. As soon as we stop playing, the pain is back though (*starts to cry*)

Connie: See you are already crying. We get like that before we pass out. Alcohol really only works to numb out for a short period of time just like the video game.

Anita: (*sobbing*) It feels so good at first. I love the high. I love the numb. It is worth it. I fucking hate life so fucking much. I hate this living just for the sake of living. I hate being this robot of just going through the motions of being human. I just fucking want to die.

Connie: (*hugging Anita*) I know, I know. Our providers say that we will feel better once we start to find some sort of purpose in this life. Drinking is not a purpose. It is an escape that doesn't last as long as we want it to. We cannot find meaning in life if we are drunk.

Anita: It is taking fucking forever for us to create a life worth living. We are fucking losers and I do not see how anything will change. I played by your rules for so long. We have been in treatment for forever and death seems to be the only solution. No more pain.

Connie: I am just as frustrated as you are that we have not really improved at all. And now here we are drinking again. What the fuck is up with that? We fucking have to keep on trying. Our providers think we can get better.

Anita: I fucking know that! I am just so fucking sick that it is taking so goddamn long to get better.

Connie: I know. It fucking sucks. The pain fucking sucks. The thought of having a life that is fulfilling feels far fetched. We want to find a job that pays well enough and one we would enjoy. That isn't going to happen. I know that as we have been looking for months and haven't gotten a job yet. Yes, this makes me want to just end it all before the debt is going to be too much to bear. I know we want to be able to make a living off of writing but that isn't going to happen either. Our life fucking sucks right now. I just think we need to tolerate it by using coping skills over the quick fixes.

Anita: The coping skills aren't strong enough.

Connie: We just need to keep finding more and more skills. We need to have some goals, something to look forward to.

Anita: We haven't found it yet. What makes you think we will find it in the future?

Connie: I don't know. There has to be something out there. We haven't always been this miserable and suicidal. We used to not mind life so much. It could come back.

Anita: That isn't a strong point. A lot of fucking variables.

Connie: I know. If we don't try at all though, we will never know if things will get better. We can be helpful to other people struggling. That is something we have always wanted to do.

Anita: We are still fucked up. I don't know how soon that will be. Probably not soon enough.

Connie: Well, I think we need to get out of this goddamn store. The alcohol has made us super depressed and I don't want to see you buying sleeping pills.

Anita: You know me well. That was going to be my next thing.

Connie: Lets buy the paints and I guess we should pay for that bottle of vodka.

Anita: I get to finish the bottle if we do.

Connie: Nope. I'm going to have them through it out.

Anita: I feel that the buzz is wearing off. I just need a few more gulps.

Connie: No you don't. We just need to get home and fucking distract ourselves. I think I'll have to call an Uber.

Anita: (*puts hand out*) Then I am definitely needing more of that vodka. Please?

Connie: (*hands over the bottle*) Fine. Whatever but this is the last fucking time.

Anita: (*drinking*) Okay. I'll give up this quick fix, I promise. I'll even try to avoid the other ones. No promises can be made though.

Connie: Deal.

CHAPTER EIGHT

Please Accept Me and Don't Leave

Abandonment and rejection are my two biggest fears. The struggle is real. I know they are two distinct fears, but they go hand in hand for me. Rejection is pre-abandonment. Abandonment is what happens if I am not instantly rejected. These two feelings do differ as rejection could happen for reasons other than striving to be liked by someone. Rejection could happen with failures at job interviews, when something I create is not received well, or when I am not told I am doing a good job at something. Abandonment is when a person I somewhat trust is mad at me, stops to contact me, or actually leaves me. Both of these feelings strike me right down to the core. I get severe pain in my chest as well as in my gut. I feel like my innards are being sucked down into a giant, bottomless canyon. I cannot shake the pain and I end up dwelling on the situation for weeks, years even. I keep replaying the situation in my head to try and figure out what I did wrong. It is not a nice place to be. I just wish my brain had an off switch.

I do understand that rejection and abandonment are a part of life. Everyone faces it. It just wraps around me like a thick fog and I cannot see things clearly. I get stuck in this spot. I have a hard time moving forward as my emotional thoughts kidnap me. Once this happens, I have almost gone past the point of no return. I cannot get out of my own way. I could have logical thoughts to counteract the emotional thoughts, but they are never strong enough. It gets me to a point where I ask myself, "Why do I even keep trying? I should leave first so I won't be abandoned. I shouldn't try in the first place so I do not have to face the rejection. The pain is unbearable. I need to abandon all hope. If I do not feel hopeful, I won't be hurt as badly." These thoughts do not help me either.

As far as abandonment is concerned, my fear always wins. For example, if I do not receive a returned text message in fifteen minutes, I assume the worst. The first thing that happens is a pain in my gut and chest. The feelings happen before I can think rationally. As it is a deep-rooted fear, I automatically have the feelings of emotional pain. I will think rational thoughts such as, "The person might be driving and cannot return the text message. I often will put my own phone on do not disturb during random times during the day, maybe she does as well. Maybe she is at work and cannot return the message." These are all logical thoughts that are quite plausible. However, my emotional thoughts will start to outweigh the logic as I am already feeling the emotional pain. "What did I do to make her mad at me? Was she never my friend to begin with? Am I being too clingy? Did she kill herself? Why am I being ignored? She hates me. I was stupid to think I could have a friend. Why did I bother? I should just kill myself." This puts me down a dark, twisted path. Once I do get a returned message, I think, "Thank God she didn't kill herself, but why is she brushing me off?" It takes a long time and multiple back and forth messages for me to be confident that I had not done something to ruin the friendship. Sometimes it is an hour, other times it is a couple of days. This scenario happens quite frequently. Logically I would think that I wouldn't be so emotional as I have been through this several times. However, my emotions cannot be tamed. A wild beast lives inside of me.

For as long as I can remember, I feared rejection and abandonment. These fears were solidified into a gigantic beast when I was in eighth grade. I always had a hard time making friends as a child. When I would have a friend, I would cling to her. She was the desk and I was the old, nasty gum stuck under her. To ensure I would be able to keep my friend, I would do what ever that friend wanted me to do. I would constantly compliment my friend. I thought, "She won't leave me as I do everything for her. I would take a detention for her if I had to."

In Steamboat Springs, Colorado it was particularly difficult to make friends. There was a core group of girls who grew up together. They were called "the get-along-gang." They rarely accepted a newbie into their clique because a lot of kids come and go in Steamboat Springs; it is a tourist town after all. When I moved there in the middle of fifth grade, I made friends with some girls who were also fairly new to the school. They befriended me and I was happy about the fact that I made friends so quickly. It turned out that they wanted my friendship as they needed someone to constantly be "it" at recess. I knew I was being used, but I had to take what I could get. I thought the pain in my gut would be worse if I didn't have these friends. At recess, I had tears dripping down my cheeks as I would count before my search. I loathed myself for this. I had friends, why was I being such a baby about the whole situation? I was used to doing what other kids told me to do. This felt different though because the friendship was only formed so they could have fun with their game. There were so many different rules in which I would never be able to come out on top. I continued to hang out with these girls as it was better than actually being physically alone like the fat kids that everyone made fun of.

Several of these girls moved away by the time sixth grade started. The one who was remaining, I clung to. Now that there was just the two of us, I could establish a true friendship. I knew how to be overly nice to people and that is what I did. We would actually talk and hang out. We were almost on equal levels with one another. She was more likable than me; therefore, I would put her on a pedestal. This is how people keep friends, right?

Of course she moved away before the start of seventh grade. I was in a total panic mode as I feared I would not have anyone. Luckily on the first day of seventh grade there was a new girl on the bus, Devon, who was also in seventh grade. I sat next to her and we became friends. She was the person I gave my locker combo to. She was the person I would invite anywhere I could. She was my skiing buddy, and I would just ski whatever trails she wanted to ski. I was the perfect friend to her. I would tell her things like she was skinny when in reality she was not. I said her ideas were brilliant. She was from a republican family. I even agreed about things she said about Ronald and Nancy Reagan. I really did not feel this way as I grew up in a very liberal household. I gave up what I believed in so I could have this friendship.

So far, it was the best relationship I had made since moving to Steamboat Springs. She recruited more friends for us to hang out with. I would always say that Devon was my best friend over and over again so no one else would swoop in and take that away from me. She is MY friend. I was jealous of the other girls, but I was friendly with them too. I did have multiple friends, but it was Devon I spent most of my time with. I feared that the common pattern of my friend moving away was going to occur again. For once, she did not move away before the beginning of eighth grade.

Eighth grade started out very well. I got used to the other girls and would joke around with them and call them on the phone. I had branched out. I still spent most of my time with Devon, but it was nice to have other options in case Devon was busy. I felt comfortable enough with the other girls that I felt it was safe in January to tell one friend, Kelsey, that a couple of other friends, Devon included, didn't think she was going to make the A team for volleyball. The A team was for the best players. I said that she needed to work on her serve according to these other girls. One would have thought that I said the two girls were planning a "Carrie" on her. Or that I said that she was not good enough and she should just give up on volleyball. Heck, I probably could have called her Hitler and wouldn't have received the backlash I had.

The morning after I had made the comment to Kelsey, my life was a living hell. I got on the bus and everyone glared at me. Devon acted like I had two heads. She was already sitting with someone else. I was very confused and found an empty seat near the younger kids. I still heard people talking about me. They were calling me a pathetic wimp. I did not know what had happened. I was fine the day before. What the hell was going on now?

When I got to school, my locker had a bunch of crap on it, deodorant I think. When I opened my locker, I found all of my pictures ripped. Devon had removed herself from the pictures we were in together, and I had some ripped pictures of myself that I had given to Devon to hang up in her locker. I tried not to cry. My chest was ripped open. I had no idea what happened between yesterday afternoon and this morning. My locker must have been destroyed during volleyball practice the night before. I broke my wrist and was not playing. This was the only time the destruction could have been done as Devon was on the bus in the morning.

An underclassman came up to me and asked if Devon ruined my locker. I replied, "probably" and then I ran to the bathroom to cry. I had gathered from the bits and pieces I had heard on the bus and the fact that all of my pictures with Devon were destroyed, was that Kelsey must have asked about why her serve was lousy. I cannot believe that this was discussed. I thought I could trust Kelsey. I guess the rule is to never tell someone what another has said behind her back. Trust no one. I was a complete idiot and I paid for it by crying in the bathroom. I had an impossible time making it to my classes. I was called names and people would spit on me as I walked down the hallways. "How can everyone be on this hatred of me so quickly?"

I just couldn't take it, and I went to the Vice Principal to say the only thing I could think of and that was that Devon had messed with my locker. Anti-bullying was not a thing back in the late 1980's. Devon ended up getting told that she was going to have to go to detention the following day at lunch and for a week after. This was a huge mistake; I let my emotions take me over and I had to do something to get back at her.

I was bullied and threatened severely at this time, and I was told by people that I had to back off on Devon and tell the Vice Principal that I forgave Devon and she shouldn't have detention. My life was going to be completely miserable if I did not do this. My new name at the school was PW which stood for pathetic wimp. Almost everyone called me that. I really wanted to scream and hit these girls. I was a prisoner to my emotions. I knew I couldn't actually fight any of the students. I would get suspended from school, and I couldn't let that happen. I backed off on the detention that Devon was supposed to get. It turned out that she still had detention for a day. I did not do what I was supposed to. I failed. I opened the door to be ridiculed more and more.

I had to stop taking the bus to school as I would be covered in spit balls and from all the people tripping me, I would get my pants filthy on the wet, mud soaked floor as there is always snow to tromp through in Steamboat Springs. I would sit in the room for detention/study hall during my lunch break to just get away from all of the teasing. This wasn't enough as I would receive phone calls at night from people telling me that everyone in the school hated me and maybe I should just die. This was the first time that suicidal thoughts came to me. I also started to hurt myself at this time. I was a complete mess. I was glad that my family was going to be moving to the East coast before I hit high school. This was one of the things that kept me alive. The other thing was making friends with Morgan, a girl who everyone always made fun of. I had always been nice to her. Someone cannot help if they have dandruff or acne. Morgan was nice. I had her to get me through the next several months. It was weird; we actually had a lot more in common than I did with Devon. I enjoyed spending time with Morgan. I did keep myself emotionally distant from her as I couldn't survive losing another close friend.

I do not know why getting bullied is not part of the ACE score. I was severely traumatized by the event. I have nightmares about it. I still have issues with being around new women now. For example, if I am in a recovery group and there are a bunch of women I do not know, I have a panic attack. I go back to repeating to myself, "I am a pathetic wimp, nobody likes me, I should just leave this group as I cannot handle the potential for the ridicule to happen again." I have held onto the lesson I learned in eighth grade, don't easily trust people and never tell someone what another said behind her back.

Oddly enough, this philosophy did not help me make friends as an adult. I guess I just thought that if the women I know are bitching about someone behind that person's back, they would do the same to me. I did not want to hear the things that would be said about another, only to hold onto the thought as I would never tell someone what was said about her. I would feel like such a phony knowing information and not being able to reveal it. It's best to not have friends like this. I was not going to play the awful game I severely lost at in middle school. I cannot be in this type of environment. It would suck the soul right out of me. I preferred to go my adult life without female friends. Jason has some friends, and it is much easier to get along with men so I just went with the flow.

My romantic relationships are riddled with abandonment issues. I always think that the person will leave me at any moment. I would get jealous if my significant other talked to people who could potentially be a lover. I had to meet the person. I had to see firsthand what the threat was. If I was denied this, I would go into full on panic and rage. I would scream and be completely out of control. My partner always had a logical reason as to why it didn't matter if I met the person or not. I retorted back that there is a huge issue. If I cannot meet this person, it must mean you are sleeping together. I would yell and throw things. I would bang my head with pots and pans. I was so enraged, and it was only imagined abandonment that got me to this place.

The craziest part is that I have cheated on everyone I was with. I was the one in the relationship who was not true. I would hide the existence of the person I was cheating with. I was doing to my partners exactly what I feared they were doing. I am actually shocked that people stayed with me as long as they have. I was not easy to get along with when the fear of abandonment dug its talons into me. Especially, when I would hold onto the fear for years after the fact. I guess my partners thought my positives outweighed my fear-provoked rage. I still do not get it.

I do not understand why Jason stays with me. I have been with him the longest and have cheated on him the most. I have fought with him hundreds of times about the same issues of jealousy over my perceived abandonment. He left his ex-wife for me. I struggled with the thought that he would go back to her for over seven years into our marriage. I knew he had to be cordial with Kelly because they have two kids together. My emotions would get the best of me, and I would feel as though I would be dumped at any moment. I would bottle up these feelings as best as I could. They would always rupture out of me and I would be a screaming, volcanic beast. I always exploded in the evenings when the kids were around. Jason, naturally, did not want to talk to me about my issues as the kids were right there. Logic had no place in my mind. I took this as a sign that my thoughts and feelings were true and he was going to leave me. This escalated the fights even more. This would lead me down a path in which I would cheat on Jason. I never slept with anyone when I cheated (aside from very recently with Amy but I was under the impression we were going with an open marriage). It was always more of an emotional attachment. I had someone to tell me positive things about myself. I thought that Jason was going to leave me anyway, maybe I could have a backup plan.

I use sex as a weapon. I would use sex to give Jason a reason to stay with me. I'm not a sexual person by nature. All of my use of sex made Jason think I was a highly sexual person, especially at the beginning of our relationship. He is a sexual being. Unfortunately, I am not. I inadvertently set this precedence that I was basically willing to have sex whenever he wanted it. I had to drink to lose my inhibitions as time went by. It took me years to finally start telling Jason that I was not interested. I thought he might leave me for this, but it was something I saw him as a demon for. It wouldn't be so bad for him to leave me now, as I hate him right now. Then I would think that I should start another emotional affair. Perhaps I could leave him first. Then I would be brought around full circle and would desperately try to not lose him. The cycle would replay over and over it was like a record getting stuck on the same groove.

Most of my violent outbursts towards Jason were in relation to fear of abandonment. I now know that he did not leave me for his ex-wife. I can still feel the pain from the days I truly thought he was leaving me as I perceived that he loved Kelly more than he loved me. Granted, he left her for me. For him, it was love at first sight. He told his friend the day he met me that he was going to leave Kelly for me. Still, my emotions insisted that he didn't truly love me. I will still feel myself traveling down the road that he might, even now after sixteen years of marriage, possibly go back to Kelly as she makes good money and I am jobless now. I understand that this is my emotion mind speaking. I try to ground myself with the reality that he is with me. He has stuck with me in spite of all of the chaos I put him through. It has to be very difficult for him to do this. I can rebuttal any factual statement with an emotion-based statement. I become a slave to my emotions. I get jealous when Jason has female friends. I do not say anything about my jealousy as I know that I would hate it if he was jealous of a male friend that I had made. Granted, my male friends always would get enthralled with me and then it turned into an emotional affair. Jason did have every right to be jealous. I know I have no right to be jealous of his situation. I am jealous though. It is just in my nature. I just need to restrain myself and not react on this jealousy. I know I am jealous because I perceive that Jason will fall for this woman and he will be cheating on me and then eventually leave me. I feel that I have it coming.

As far as rejection, abandonment's twin sister, is concerned, I feel the same intense emotions. Rejection can be the average rejection anyone would feel such as getting fired from a job or not getting a new job. Rejection could be not having a poem accepted in a publication. Again, this is a reasonable feeling to have I couldn't imagine anyone disputing my feelings that I am a loser because I didn't get what I wanted to. As these are everyday feelings for everyone. For me, however, rejection goes far beyond these obvious forms.

I feel rejected as my best friend, Shannon, from high school has moved to another state and has made new close friends. Logically, I know that Shannon did not leave me. She is living somewhere where she is able to work the job she longed for. She's moved to a place that isn't far from her husband's family. I know she has moved on as we are adults now. Emotionally, however, I feel like she doesn't care for me anymore as she has a new best friend. I shed tears when I see that she is having a great time with her new friends on Facebook. I feel like I am not good enough anymore. I feel like I was not a true friend. I feel like I had done something wrong. Of course all of these feelings are ludicrous. I am still friends with Shannon. Here, twenty years later, when we get together, we laugh uncontrollably and it was like no time had passed since we use to hang out on a daily basis. My rational mind knows that I have nothing to fear. I was not rejected because she moved away and has new friends. I mean what adult would still cling to having the one best friend from high school and not teeter from that? Well, me I guess. I am unique though, or is it that I'm crazy? Six of this, half dozen of the other. I feel rejected as she has moved on with her life. I do not feel abandoned as we do still chat. I just feel rejected as I was thrown off the throne of being Shannon's best friend. She is still my best friend and this should be enough for me. I feel ridiculous for crying over the fact that Shannon is happy and has new friends to share this joy with. Shannon is an absolutely amazing person, and I like seeing that she is doing well in life. My perceived rejection is the knife I twist in my gut. My logical side goes off-line and I am stuck with my emotions and the thoughts that follow closely behind the feelings. I have to keep telling myself that my emotions do not equal reality.

As I am writing this book, I am experiencing intense feelings of rejection. My mind keeps playing the tape over and over again, "I'm not good enough. This is a stupid idea. Why did I even bother? No one will ever read it. Just stop writing right now as the book will go no where. I'm an idiot for putting myself out there to be ridiculed and rejected. Maybe I should just kill myself now so I won't have to go through the inevitable rejection." Why do I continue to write then? I guess I have to say that I have some sort of hope. I have a love/hate relationship with hope. The thing is, hope will keep me moving forward. However, if I feel hopeful that something will happen such as getting a job and I am rejected, my soul is ripped from my body. An earthquake tears through my chest, leaving a hollow, empty, gapping hole. I then hate the fact that hope seduced me with her siren call. Hope, unfortunately, usually plays a negative role in my life. She gets me to try but then when I fail I curse her name and want to just give up.

I feel rejection when I perceive that a provider doesn't like me anymore. I fear that the provider will leave me. It had happened before. Of course my therapists left as they moved out of state. I still felt like they were abandoning me. I know, it's ridiculous, as they obviously didn't move out of state because they didn't want to work with me anymore. If I truly thought that, then I would also be thinking that the world revolves around me. No logic is involved with the evil twins abandonment and rejection.

Recently, I did feel rejected by Dr. Price. My rational side vanished like a fart in the wind. I decided that I would stop my treatment all together. I figured it would be easier for me to leave than to be abandoned. I needed to rebuttal rejection with rejection. I am actually still in the throws of this as I write this November 15th, 2018. I decided I needed to write a psycho-scribble piece to help me come to terms with my thoughts and feelings. The piece showed me what I feel like happens when I am in this panicked state. It has brought me understanding. I am going to use this clarity to move on and put the pieces back together. I wrote a short skit of a conversation between my rational side and my emotional/irrational side. I did not come around to wise mind in the writing, but I was able to see in print why I get so seemingly crazy in these situations.

If you want to write something similar, I suggest you create some sort of scene with conflict. The fact that conflict is already established in the scene will make it easier for the two sides of yourself to be honest and just let it all out. Of course this suggestion is based on the personification of the two sides. It doesn't have to be personified like how I write my pieces. It could be writing down a conversation with yourself. Once you "hear" both sides of the story, it can help bring clarity. If nothing else, it will give you something different to write about in your journal. If it doesn't bring you to any clarity, then at least you have acknowledged the two opposing sides and gave them each a voice. You will have planted the seed and in the future maybe you can circle back and water the plant.

Scene starts out black. The lights come on as the first words are spoken. It is a room that has no doors. The walls are pained with various colors. One wall is pink and pastel blue with images of hearts, rainbows, butterflies and soft fluffy clouds. The second wall is red and it has crooked black lines randomly painted throughout, there are also lots of orange flames with blue centers. The third wall is grey and brown with a huge black canyon in the middle of it. The fourth wall is black and there is a small image of a woman on her side in the fetal position with tears flowing down her face creating a crevice that is filled with tears that extends down to the bottom of the wall. There are two women. Rational "Randi" and irrational/emotional "Irene". Randi is tied up to a chair which is the only piece of furniture in the room. Irene is adding another flame to the second wall. (11/10/18)

Randi: (*slowly waking up as the lights come on, her head is still down*) What the fuck?

Irene: Hey, sleepy head.

Randi: (*fully alert and tries to get her hands out of the ropes behind her back*) Shit! We are here. Fuck me. What happened?

Irene: (*dropping her paint brush to the floor*) You passed out so I tied you up for safety.

Randi: Bullshit! Untie me now. What did you do to me?

Irene: (*nonchalantly*) Okay, I knocked you out. I had to. I had to tie you to the chair to keep you safe.

Randi: Fuck, me! What is it this time? Love? We were wronged? Please don't…

Irene: (*interrupting*) Abandonment and rejection.

Randi: Shit. You aren't going to untie me are you?

Irene: Nope.

Randi: I cannot get out of this doorless room. You are the only one who can get me out of here. Just be nice and untie me.

Irene: No can do, girlfriend. I am steering the ship now.

Randi: Well what the fuck happened? You knocked me out so I have no idea what is going on.

Irene: Perfect, the less you know the better it is.

Randi: You cannot keep locking me up in your space. I need to have a say in this before it gets too chaotic.

Irene: (*wrapping her arms around Randi's shoulders to whisper in Randi's ear*) I am completely correct on this one. We should be pissed. We don't need you to make up some sort of bull crap justifying it.

Randi: Fuck, are you saying it is real? We really were abandoned?

Irene: All signs point to yes. (*she dances across the stage*)

Randi: All signs? What are the signs? I need to know!

Irene: I thought I was supposed to be the emotional one. Maybe being in my room is good for you.

Randi: You aren't answering my question.

Irene: I don't have to. There is nothing for you to worry about. I have this handled.

Randi: What are we doing to our self right now? You know I am completely blocked off in here.

Irene: We had first tried a bunch of different distractions but they didn't last long. Now we are cutting and we left a nasty voice-mail. My angry side was in control there.

Randi: Jesus, that is not under control. Untie me and maybe I can help bring some ration...

Irene: (interrupting) I will let you go when everything smooths over.

Randi: Smooths over? It already sounds like we are in too deep.

Irene: Baby, you know that we always dive in too deep when it comes to being abandoned.

Randi: Just because I am aware of the pattern doesn't mean I have to accept it.

Irene: Well, I have you trapped, so you better accept it.

Randi: Who was it? Who left us?

Irene: It is too painful to talk about.

Randi: You fucking love talking about pain and despair. Why won't you tell me?

Irene: Again, the less you know, the

Randi: (interrupting) What? The better it is? For who?

Irene: For us, silly.

Randi: What if you are wrong? What if you are just perceiving abandonment?

Irene: I am not wrong. I know what the situation is and its bad. If we use logic, it is only going to prove my point more.

Randi: Fine, I just need to know who it is. You cannot keep me trapped in your space forever. I'm going to be needed so we don't do something rash and possibly end up in jail.

Irene: Jail won't be an issue.

Randi: Is it Jason? Did he finally decide to dump our crazy cheating ass? Fuck!

Irene: No, it's not Jason.

Randi: You are a lousy fucking driver. Let me go so I can figure this shit out.

Irene: You would ruin it.

Randi: Ruin what? The suffering? The broken relationship?

Irene: Yes.

Randi: Yes, what?

Irene: Yes, you would get us to believe that we are safe and not being left. You would give us a false sense of hope. I cannot handle that shit on top of what is currently going on.

Randi: So, you are saying that the abandonment and rejection isn't set in stone then? Well, fuck.

Irene: I feel like it is set in stone. It is an intuitive thing. The pain in our gut should be enough to prove to you that it is real.

Randi: I wish I could read your fucking mind. I should be able to do that.

Irene: If we were able to read each others minds, I think we would be stable. Too balanced, you know. Stable is boring. We need excitement.

Randi: Yes, we need excitement because fuck boredom. Couldn't we go to an amusement park and ride some crazy rides?

Irene: We could do that and gamble and maybe skydive. But that is not enough to scratch our itch. We need a little chaos.

Randi: A little chaos is fine. But when you are in charge it is total chaos. (*trying to free her hands*)

Irene: You aren't going to be able to loosen that rope. You will just waste your energy. We might be in my space for days.

Randi: I cannot take being in here for that long. I cannot handle not knowing what is even going on with us! Fucking blind spot. I hate this room. I fucking hate you sometimes.

Irene: It's only sometimes? That's cool. I can live with that.

Randi: Shut up. Tell me what is going on.

Irene: Well the pit in our chest is trying to be filled with sweets and self harm. The pain is unbearable. We are thinking that suicide might be the only answer.

Randi: Jesus, you said earlier that this abandonment is not set in stone, just your feeling of it was. Now we are thinking of killing ourself?

Irene: You inferred that I said it wasn't set in stone. Remember, honey, I'm raw. Feelings are all I have to go off of. So killing ourself or go back to being a drunk again seems like the only option. Because this loss is so fucking bad!

Randi: If it isn't Jason, then who is it?

Irene: Someone we desperately need in our lives.

Randi: Did one of the kids run away?

Irene: Oh, God, no. Could you imagine? We would definitely be really drunk right now if that was the case. Or dead. Yeah, I am thinking dead.

Randi: Is it our friend with benefits? Has she moved on? Because if that is the case, I could see us being disappointed. It is not the end of the world though. We are the ones who are married and not actually available. It was fun while it lasted.

Irene: No, it's not Amy. There was a little jealousy when someone else has been chatting with her. Nothing major.

Randi: (*slowly trying to loosen the rope*) We were jealous of that? Shit. Goddamn rejection and abandonment. I fucking hate how it gets us so easily. Of course, you are the major one to blame for that.

Irene: I know. It's in our nature, though. Past traumatic events never help. We just naturally put me in charge. It's an automatic response.

Randi: That is your doing though. I never voted to put you in charge. You decided years ago that you are the president over abandonment and rejection.

Irene: I am a good president. This is my world. You have no place here. I am sick of hearing about your justifications. They never do us any good. That's why I have to kidnap you.

Randi: (*still working at rope*) You did not gag me. You must want to hear what I have to say on the matter.

Irene: I didn't gag you because I like the company.

Randi: I would be better company if you untied me.

Irene: You know I cannot do that.

Randi: (*still working on the rope*) You are capable of untying me. You just don't want to. How about this, if you untie me, I will not interfere the next time we run into a passive aggressive, asshole driver.

Irene: That's a laugh. You rarely step in for that. Your logic knows the other driver is wrong. I don't think you care if I yell and flip the driver off. I rarely fight back with aggression anymore, that's what you really cannot stand.

Randi: Touché. What if I step back from your need to flirt all of the time with anyone who says something nice. I'll let you go full on flirt.

Irene: I like that option better, but still, no.

Randi: (*still trying to get free*) You, bitch!

Irene: I'm not going to let you ruin this. We have already made certain decisions based on the circumstance. I don't want to look like an idiot by going back on what I decided.

Randi: I won't fucking ruin it! I need to know the facts. What is going on? What decisions did we make?

Irene: We will be stopping treatment.

Randi: What? Please say it was DBT only. I agree that shit doesn't work well.

Irene: No, we have to stop it all.

Randi: Because of the lack of insurance?

Irene: That is a piece of the puzzle.

Randi: So, one of our providers decided that they didn't want to work with us anymore. That has to be it.

Irene: (*awkwardly*) Ah, no. Why would you think? Shit. Fine. You got me. Yes, Dr. Price is going to leave us.

Randi: Fuck, no. What did you do? Did he actually say he was leaving us?

Irene: He did not say the words directly.

Randi: Well what the fuck did he say?

Irene: Ok, so get this. In one breath he says that he will continue to work with us as long as we need it. In another breath he says he doesn't like us.

Randi: Why doesn't he like us? What did you do?

Irene: It's probably because we are too clingy. We are also so fucking boring right now. I think we make everyone want to hit themselves with a bat as we cannot hold an interesting and intelligent conversation.

Randi: (*almost has hands free from the rope*) Did he tell us to stop calling him and writing him letters? I call bullshit on being too boring. We have too much shit going on.

Irene: No, HE didn't say that we should stop calling him when we are in crisis, etc. In my angry voicemail, I told him that we would leave him alone. He apparently doesn't give a shit about us. We are unlikeable. I just want to make his job easier on him.

Randi: (*still freeing herself*) How long was I passed out? Christ.

Irene: About a day or two.

Randi: Shit. You need to tell me what was said exactly. It sounds like there will be a lot of mending to do. The abandonment part turned out to be bullshit. Makes me think the rejection might be imagined as well.

Irene: I know what I felt when he spoke. It was that empty pain. This isn't imagined.

Randi: (finally has her hands free) I did not ask what you felt numb nut. You always feel. That is your fucking job. I need to know the exact words.

Irene: (looking at the wall with the woman who is all alone) Trust me. Reading between the lines, it is as clear as day that he doesn't like us as a person.

Randi: (untying her legs) Reading between the lines? I agree that needs to be done sometimes. I need the whole fucking story here or I cannot come up with a logical answer.

Irene: (still staring at wall) It's too late. We are trying to get out of the house with a bunch of pills to die in a hotel bathtub.

Randi: (standing up) It's not too late. You said we are trying to get out. That means we aren't out yet. (slowly walking up behind Irene)

Irene: Yeah, Jason checked out our bag and he took it away from us, the keys too.

Randi: Well shit, it sounds like we are in for the night then.

Irene: We are still trying but a threat of being brought to the ER was made. I think we are stuck and will have to take our evening meds early.

Randi: (*wrapping her arms around Irene*) Please tell me what was said. If we are just going to be sleeping soon anyway, just tell me now. If we are asleep, neither of us has control.

Irene: Please get your arms off of me. I know that Dr. Price told us that we aren't liked. Again, it was not in those words directly, but I know it was said. My emotional upheaval was so intense. I know it was based on validity.

Randi: I have also been telling you that our crush on him isn't logical at all. We know for a fact that we will never be with him. There are hundreds of reasons why. Still, you go on.

Irene: I know. I just cannot help those feelings. This not being liked is different though It is a greater pain than holding onto love that will never be reciprocated.

Randi: Perhaps you were more vulnerable because of those feelings? Maybe you twisted things way out of proportion? The words, please.

Irene: He found it frightening that we wanted to kill ourself because of a scheduling error. He said he would continue to work with us. We spoke of thinking we were going to be dropped as a patient because we had made some bad decisions and he seemed disappointed in us the previous week. This is why I thought the scheduling error was something done on purpose so he would stop seeing us.

Randi: You saw it was an error and not an abandonment. Right?

Irene: Eventually, I guess. I still feel like it might happen, though.

Randi: What did he say exactly that made you feel like he hates us?

Irene: Well, in relation to wanting to die as a result of a scheduling error, and the fact I felt for sure we were being dropped as a patient, he said that the goal of treatment isn't for a provider to like you.

Randi: (*squeezing on Irene tighter*) He was probably talking as a generalization.

Irene: (*crying*) No, I know he was talking about not liking us.

Randi: Well, shit. I can tell that we are falling asleep, pills do work. We probably won't get any further tonight. Any chance you let me out of your space before the time of dreams?

Irene: (*brushing a tear off and smiles*) You are funny. Thanks for putting a smile on my face.

Several Hours Later

Randi: Okay, we are awake now. Could I please be freed so I can try to help repair this?

Irene: And a good morning to you, too.

Randi: Shut up. I know we are awake I just don't know what is going on with us.

Irene: We are miserable and isolating. We are angry with Jason. We will be making the calls soon to cancel therapy and seeing Dr. Price for next week. We have already decided to skip DBT.

Randi: Well fuck. We still want to die I am assuming.

Irene: Most definitely. We don't have the pills we will have to go out and buy new ones. However we are feeling too depressed to go out to a store.

Randi: It sounds like you need to let me out. Things are going downhill fast.

Irene: Yes, they are. But it is unstoppable. We are leaving a message right now to cancel our appointments. The decision has been made. I cannot let you out of here until I know it will be safe to do so.

Randi: Safe to do so? What is that supposed to mean?

Irene: I cannot have you calling Dr. Price back to apologize for the previous voicemail. I cannot have you questioning the validity that he doesn't like us.

Randi: Why? What is the harm in that?

Irene: We would look like a fool. We specifically said we weren't going to call anymore. Plus, if you ask if we are hated and the answer is yes, we are hated, you know we will do something crazy. I am not sure what, but it will probably be destructive.

Randi: Fine, I promise. If I get out of here I won't drive for a little bit. I will not make a phone call. I just want to be able to get through to us, try to rationalize that we haven't been kicked out of treatment. We are deciding to stop treatment and maybe I could change our mind. Just talking to you doesn't get me anywhere. I have no power what so ever in here.

Irene: Just give me a couple of hours and I will set you free. Jason is yelling at us right now for stopping treatment. I don't want you to cave in and crawl on your hands and knees back into treatment. You seem to see value in it.

Randi: What's so wrong about going to treatment? Other than the fact that it isn't helping as much as I think it should be. Also, it has made the job search thing a bit more difficult I will admit.

Irene: If we back down, it will show that we are weak. I do not want us seen as weak. Especially as Jason is giving us such a hard time about it right now. I don't want to call back to reschedule appointments. We need to prove to him that we are strong. We need to be mad at him for stopping us from leaving the house with the pills. We need to show that we can make our own decisions.

Randi: Fuck. This was your fucking decision and not mine. We did not collaborate at all on this one. It's bullshit. Our best decisions are the ones we make together. I had no choice in this matter. You knocked me out and brought me to your room that I cannot get out of. You fucking tied me to a chair. You are too fucking emotional to be driving right now. I need to help. Let me take the wheel. Please. Use the love you are capable of and set me free.

Irene: Shhh. There's a new development. Jason is kicking us out. He's threatening to call the cops on us and have a protection from abuse order thrown on us. We keep calling his bluff, of course, as we need to gather our things if we are getting kicked out. Jason has now called Dr. Price. That was a dick move.

Randi: I agree on that. Dick move. I cannot imagine what is going on in his head.

Irene: Shit, we were just handed the phone. We have to speak.

Randi: Hey, we didn't make the call. Jason did. Let's both escape this room and handle the call together. Come on. I know you are too emotional to handle this call very well. Please, let me help you.

Irene: Shit, I am fucking bombing out here. Fine I will release you. You need to take the call.

Randi: Thanks. I'll figure out where we left off on the conversation. This is good. Dr. Price is talking. I guess he never said anything close to the fact that he hated us. He said that providers need to like the patient in the first month of treatment. If they don't, they have to figure out what they are going to do then. Liking a patient is needed in treatment. It's our reaction to needing to be liked is the issue.

Irene: I am not stuck in your room. I hear everything that is being said. Why are you telling him that we will see him next Wednesday?

Randi: It's because he doesn't hate us and we could use the session after all of this crap.

Irene: Fine. I still don't want to do DBT. I also want therapy to stop. Get off of meds Just go back to the times before therapy. Maybe drink a ton again. We cannot afford treatment anymore and will be broke in no time. Too much anxiety for me.

Randi: Well, maybe we could play it by ear.

Irene: I'll agree to that. I cannot believe that Jason is actually kicking us out of the house.

Randi: I know, right? I guess Jason is sticking to his guns and putting up strong boundaries.

Irene: I want to stick to my guns of giving up.

Randi: We said we are going to play it by ear. If it seems like the treatment isn't going anywhere as we are not getting measurably better, I will agree to end it all after we see Dr. Price on Wednesday.

Irene: Good. You still won't persuade us to go to DBT will you?

Randi: Hey, lady. The last time we wanted to quit, you said you would go because Dr. Price told you to and your feelings took over.

Irene: Shut up. I can't help it.

Randi: You shouldn't have knocked me out. We could have been very reasonable in this situation.

Irene: Well, it already happened. No going back. I now need to figure out what emotion to use as we are staying at Amy's. The friend's with benefits thing has gone to a whole new level.

Randi: Just don't throw your whole body into what ever emotion it is. Tread lightly for once. Don't lock me up. I will help you.

Irene: Thanks. Just know I cannot control myself very well and I will be knocking you out time and time again.

Randi: I know. If I can step in before you get out of control, I will. We put each other through shit, but we need each other.

Irene: Truth. Peace out.

CHAPTER NINE

Tell Me I'm Good, Tell Me I'm Good

The need for validation from others is something I have struggled with all of my life. I couldn't tell myself I had done well with something. I think I was born without the part of the brain where you can validate yourself. I needed someone else to acknowledge and praise me. If I accomplished a task and no one noticed, I would see myself as a complete failure. If I am not praised, I am a nobody. As I got older, I needed more than one person telling me that I was doing well. I need more than one person telling me I am attractive, intelligent, nice or... I could go on forever here. I thought what if this one person is lying to me? I needed more people to confirm the truth. I have something well beyond co-dependence. I have multiple dependence. I know that's not a thing, but it feels like it to me. I would give anything to be able to believe one person's praise. Heck, I wish I could validate myself. That would be the best option, but I am having a really hard time doing so. I am working on it, but miracles do not grow on trees.

I do not know when this need became so much a part of my life. All I know is that it happened at a very young age. By elementary school, I needed friends to tell me I was likable. Of course they didn't put it in that many words. Come on now, we were like seven. Of course, I did not know that I was seeking acknowledgement and validation. I had figured this much out about myself by the time I had reached middle school.

I did not know how to go about making friends as a child. I ended up being friends with the two smartest and bossiest girls in the school. No one else liked them because they were smarty-pants power trippers. Again, not in so many words, let's not get ahead of ourselves here, kids don't think like that. The friendships were a win-win situation; they wanted to tell somebody what to do and I wanted to be liked. The only issue was when the three of us got together it was a tug-of-war for me to do things for them. I never had to think on my own; it was being done for me. Man, those were the days. I just had to act. I knew I was not happy. However, as a needy child, I did what I had to. I needed to be liked. I needed to know that I was real. Often I would feel detached from my body. I would not recognize myself in the mirror. Who is this hollow shell of a person staring back at me? Did either of my friends acknowledge me today? No? I guess I am not real. Oh wait, we spoke on the phone, I am real.

I definitely needed validation from my parents. I wanted to do well in school so I could hear the praise. I would do my chores to the best of my ability to gain positive acknowledgement. Usually I would do what I was told, so I could be told I had done a good job. I wanted my back patted when I would not hit my younger brother. That never happened; I only got into trouble when I did hit him. I thought I had been good by not striking him, where was my acknowledgement? Without the positive reinforcement, I would go back to being mean to my younger brother. I mean, why the heck not? No one told me I was good for not doing it. So I would be violent to gain acknowledgment of my existence. It is heart wrenching to have to rely on others opinions. This is just a part of who I am and I need to accept it.

As I grew older, I relied on my grades to validate me. After moving halfway across the country in ninth grade, I did poorly in school. I was depressed and the schools out east are more difficult than the schools in the mid-west. I beat myself up constantly for this factor. I could not believe how stupid I had become. I had to get my head out of my ass and start spending a lot of time on homework. I had pulled my grades up and finally felt like I wasn't an idiot. It was at this time I found that I loved creative writing. I used to make up stories in my head as a kid all of the time and now I was just putting my stories on paper. It was something I enjoyed doing, but if I was not being complemented on the writing I think I would have stopped doing it.

My first healthy relationship I had outside of my family was with my best friend, Shannon. We met in ninth grade. We both had similar senses of humor and enjoyed a lot of the same things. This relationship really made me feel validated. She would constantly laugh at the things I said. We would work on things together such as putting together a homemade music video. This was in the days that MTV actually played music videos. We would do almost everything together. Was I co-dependent in this relationship? It is hard to say. I definitely spent more time with Shannon than I did with either of the guys I dated. I really wasn't into dating much anyway. I just did it so I would be called beautiful. Shannon validated me for my humor, creativity, intelligence, and likability. I think the only reason why I survived my high school years was because of Shannon and my writing.

College was a positive experience for me, mostly. I started out as a creative writing major. It was a very select program where they would only accept fifteen students to go for this BFA. I was involved with theatre and the LBGTQ club. I made a couple of friends, but I was not as close to them as I was to Shannon. My female friends were basically glorified acquaintances. I found that I could relate better with the guys. Naturally, I spent time with these guys as they were validating me. I was too naive to see that they just wanted to hook up with me. The movie, *There's Something About Mary*, was my life my freshman year of college. One week all three of my male friends told me that they were in love with me. Due to my need for validation, I was flattered. However, I did not want to be with any of them. I was in a tough spot. My emotions told me to just keep it up, just continue to lead these guys on. It made me feel good to be wanted by three people. I must not be a bad person if three guys fell in love with me. However, my rational mind told me that I was going to have to tell the truth that I just wanted to be friends. It would be cruel of me to keep them on a leash. I knew what I had to do but then I would lose my validity. I did eventually tell them all that I just wanted to be friends. I felt a knife twisting in my gut. That was my emotional mind grieving for the loss of being desired. I now had my taste of what it felt like to have this three-fold validation. I liked it. I wanted more of the same, but I really did not want it to be at the expense of others. My rational mind and emotion mind fight about this all of the time. It's a ping-pong match.

My first significant relationship I had during my college years was with a woman and I was twenty-one. She was constantly giving me praise and brought me into her world. I was now friends with her friends. I felt like I had a place. I thought, oh maybe I'm a lesbian and that is why I always led guys on only to deny them when they asked for sex. I thought maybe I do not need to be loved by multiple people. I just need to be loved by a woman. That feeling did not last long. After time, I grew bored and needed someone else to tell me I was great and hot. I ended up cheating on my girlfriend a year into the relationship. I cheated on her with a guy who I knew liked me and he was not looking for a relationship. I broke down and had sex with him as I really wanted to be loved by multiple people. I could not believe that I had sex with a guy I was only acquainted with through theatre. At that point, I didn't care. I had to take it to the next level as my need for others approval only got stronger as I grew older.

I had started a pattern and would end up cheating on everyone else I would date. The cheating would be with women or men. I figured out I was bisexual. Somehow I would justify in my mind that it was okay to cheat if I hooked up with a guy when I was dating a woman. Or if I hooked up with a woman as I dated a guy. I like the best of both worlds, and no single person could give me this. I know it was wrong to think this way. My emotion mind had won the arm wrestling match with my rational mind and I stuck to the belief.

I thought that once I got married to Jason that this behavior of mine would go away. He loved me enough to marry me, so I must be an okay person. This thought lasted for a bit. However, I was extremely jealous of his ex-wife, and this caused me to do a lot of irrational things based out of emotion. Whenever a guy paid attention to me, I was like, oh good a friend. I know deep down that there was more to it then that. I am a siren. I cannot help leading people on, only to cause them to crash. The guilt I felt for having an emotional affair with kissing did not outweigh my need for validation. I also felt guilty as I was misleading these guys and once a woman. I had to think that my gain of approval from someone other than Jason was more important than the pain I would cause. I was addicted to being lusted after.

Jason would often ask me why other people's opinion about me mattered more than his. I said that it did not matter more than his opinion, I just need others to like me. He has a hard time with this. It makes sense. My opinion of him is all that he needs. He doesn't care what other people think. He can also validate himself. I think he just cannot grasp how real it is to me to be desired by multiple people. I wish I was not this way but I am.

Rationally, I can see how ridiculous it is to need others to tell me that I am a good person. If I do not have any friends, I am a boring, worthless individual. If I do not get praised at work for accomplishing a task, I am incompetent and stupid. If a straight man or lesbian walking down the street doesn't check me out, I must be hideous. These are all tapes that play in my head. My lack of self-acceptance is deeply rooted in my belief system. Knowing that my emotional half really takes over in this department, I have to really step back and examine myself.

The writing activity I ended up doing was a stand-up act. Dr. Price had suggested this type of writing to me when I was having a hard time with anxiety. He said if I could add some humor to the emotional thoughts that maybe it would not seem as intense. Through humor, he thought I could gain a different kind of clarity. I took his idea from August 2018 to write the following stand-up skit in late October 2018. I rationllally know how ludicrous it is to need to approval from other people. I think I am terrible or I do not exist without the validation. I tried to go the humor route to point out to my emotional mind that she's kinda crazy with this need of hers. This psychoscribble piece was a very difficult one for me to do. I actually had to re-write it in its entirety as my emotional mind was like, girlfriend, I am the one who is correct here. Let me win. It was definitely an emotional-mind-takes-over script. With great sorrow, I aborted this writing. I know I said I wasn't editing my psychoscribble but in this circumstance I had to as my original was a toxic piece. Both sides need their story told. We have emotion mind and rational mind for a reason. These two have to come together to see clarity. Adding humor to something is rarely a bad thing.

If you do decide to go the humor route with one of your thoughts or emotions, I say do it in any way that works for you. There are definitely certain feelings I have that I would never be able to add comedy to. As stated above, I was told to write a stand-up act for a different emotion and I couldn't bring myself to do it. I wrote some terrible jokes in my stand-up routine as I want it to feel real to me. It might have been better if I just stuck with my emotion mind versus my rational mind. I wrote it in a way that ended up working for me. I had to set up as a whole scene that I could picture in my mind.

If you think that writing humor is not for you, then simply don't do it. You could make any circumstance lighter using other methods such as compassion. I know it is difficult for me to use self compassion. Different things work for different people. The point is to find new ways of looking at things and having structured ideas to get it out on paper.

I am human, and therefore I was nervous about having a publisher look at this manuscript. I do have a part of me who has confidence. My confidence still needs outside validation. I wrote a piece about my nerves of waiting to hear back for the publisher. The piece could very well have been incorporated into my anxiety chapter. I think it actually serves best in this chapter. I can validate myself well enough to know that I do have a talent for writing. However, I always need someone else telling me that I am good. This piece is just a scene without humor incorporated into it.

The set up is a small stage with a stool and a microphone. It is a very small comedy club. Desperately seeking validity "Valerie" is ready to come up on stage. This is her first performance. There are several tables littered with empty beer bottles and an audience that is fairly lit.

John: I'd like to introduce you to Valerie's debut performance. She is authentic and crass.

Applause.

Valerie: Thanks, John. I would have said, welcome Debbie Downer to the stage. Now these poor people have no idea what their two drink minimum is actually going to cost them.

A few giggles.

Valerie: That wasn't funny. Or was it? I don't know. I need you to laugh at me or I will kill myself at the end of the night. So thank you.

Several people in the audience: Boo.

A man: I thought you were supposed to be crass. Say something funny.

Valerie: Your wife is ugly.

Man: She's my sister you whore.

Valerie: You think I'm attractive enough to be a whore? I guess the lighting is really poor in here. Thanks, anyway. I think your sister is cute. I'd do her.

Man: You are a fox. I don't remember this evening being called pity party comedy.

Giggles.

Valerie: Speaking of ugly, I have to have quite a few drinks before I find myself attractive enough so I can masturbate. I look in the mirror, hmm? I am fairly drunk. Am I drunk enough to do THAT though?

Laughter.

Valerie: Sometimes I tried before I got shit faced. Fucking waste of my time. My fingers prune and I still don't get off.

Laughter.

Valerie: Ladies? High five? No? None of you can relate to finger pruning? Great, just like my orgasm I am left here hanging.

Giggles.

Valerie: I am glad you guys can laugh at my pain. The struggle is real. Anyway, I got sober about a year ago.

Applause.

Valerie: Thank you. I perceived myself to be a lot funnier when I was a drunk. Of course the joke of pretending that everything with a handle was a dick probably got old for everyone but myself. It's funny when Adam Sandler does it.

Giggles.

Valerie: Why are you chuckling? I was saying I wasn't funny. Is this just a pity reach around as you are fucking me in the ass?

Giggles.

The sister: Coming off as needy isn't a good look for a comic. I'm ready to take this strap-on off and shove the dildo down your throat.

Laughter.

Valerie: I'll take it. At least you need to touch me to shove a shit covered dildo down my throat.

Groans and a few laughs.

Valerie: You know when you don't feel real?

Silence.

Valerie: Really? None of you ever thought am I real? No? Okay, when I feel that way I just turn around in an elevator and ask everybody when was the last time they had masturbated. They all either look up or down and I never get an answer. So I am thinking, oh I am not real. I can piss on this elevator floor and get away with it. FINALLY!

Giggles.

Valerie: But once I start pissing, I am called a lunatic. Not sure why it took that extreme to acknowledge my existence. Indecent exposer makes one real. Who knew? I guess I can skip the conversation the next time I feel like a zombie and just go streaking.

Giggles.

A man: I don't know if you are real.

Laughter.

Valerie: (*Starts to take off her shirt*) Wait a minute. You almost got me. You wouldn't like what you saw anyway. My bra fits me on better backwards. A small strap to cover my nipples and good support for my shoulder blades.

Laughter.

Man: Prove it!

Valerie: You, sir must be drunker than an Irish man on St. Patty's day. How long is my window of time before you become too sober to do me?

Man: You are hot. I don't get why you are saying you are so ugly. As long as it is just a fuck, I can handle crazy.

Valerie: Are you shitting me? I'm old and hideous.

Man: Dry that out and plant a garden.

Laughter.

Valerie: It is hard to make friends as an adult. As a toddler, all you had to do was share a toy and then you were BFFs for the rest of the day. Now I strike up a conversation and have a friend for ten minutes. Where did having a friend for the day go?

A woman: Buy me a drink and I'll be your BFF for the rest of the evening.

Valerie: Oh, buying things for people is where I am going wrong. Should have known as I pay a therapist to be my friend. Sure, I'll by you a drink.

A man: Next round of drinks is on Valerie.

Cheers.

Valerie: I am desperate to be liked but I am not that desperate. Or am I? Where is my paid for friend? She would tell me an answer.

Man: (*chants*) You are desperate, you are desperate.

Valerie: I don't have a job. I am needy but not an imbecile. Speaking of dumb, you know when you question your intelligence?

A woman: I can see how you would.

Laughter.

Woman: I did not mean you are stupid, I meant that you have no self esteem, girl.

A man: Why did you even decide to become a comedian if you don't think you are funny or attractive or real even?

Valerie: I'm a masochist.

Man: You just woke up one day and said heck, I'll go up on stage and say bad things about myself? Then I'll go home and pour hot wax on myself?

Valerie: No, I have to have some hope that I will be liked. If you cannot like yourself you need someone else to do it. And now we are back to me stinking up the stage being a total downer.

Woman: Yeah get back to talking about why you think you're dumb. Or no it was questioning if you are dumb.

Valerie: Right, my tiny brain almost forgot. I used to sneak into high school classes and would answer as many questions as I could. If I answered the most questions accurately in the class, I must be smart. However, unlike in 90210, adults playing teenagers doesn't actually work in real life.

Giggles.

Valerie: I have been banned from every school in the state. So now I walk around and ask people if the square route of twenty-five is five? They look at me like I am crazy.

Woman: You are fucking crazy, why the fuck is my opinion about you better than your own opinion about yourself? Just saying.

Giggles.

Valerie: Because it's a need of mine, like a bicycle needs a chain. Like a homeless person needs a shower. Like a fire needs a match… I could go on and on.

Woman: But what if my opinion is shit? What do you do then?

Valerie: Someone else's shit smells better than my own.

Giggles.

Man: You bought that woman a drink. Do the rest of us have invalidating opinions of you?

Cheers and applause.

Valerie: Oh, shit. Did I buy her a drink? I didn't realize the words coming out of my mouth were believed. I guess a flower grew out of my bullshit. I should have trusted myself and not walked right into that one. I'm not very trust worthy though. Fuck my life. Round of drinks on me.

Cheers.

Valerie: Six dollar limit. Goddamn, I am pathetic.

A woman: Being pathetic, maybe, you desperately trying to be liked, definitely.

Valerie: I think I am addicted to self-sabotage and imploding now that I don't have the booze.

A man: Get back to your routine. Looking pretty and buying us drinks is not going to earn you any true respect.

Valerie: Job interviews, they suck right?

A woman: Don't give up on finding a day job!

Giggles.

A man: I agree, you are funny, but you are the worst comic ever. Your self-pity act bites and coming to a comedy club is not a place to look for friends.

Giggles.

Valerie: Okay, what eves. The interviewer is like do you want this job selling crap to gullible individuals? I'm like fuck no. I mean, yes I do. I don't know why I don't get hired. Was it something I said?

Giggles.

Valerie: In all seriousness, if you think you are shit and need others to validate you are not shit, it's a tough go in an interview. These people don't want to tell you that you are good. They want you to do it yourself. And I'm thinking, what? I have to participate?

A few claps.

Valerie: They ask me what I did well at my previous job. I'm like handling customer escalations, maybe? I don't know. What do you think? Tell me I'm hired. And then I get on my hands and knees and beg, please the job is shit, I am shit, just hire me.

One chuckle.

Valerie: Sorry, I am totally off script here. I didn't like what I wrote so I ripped it up. I thought being on stage was going to bring me to a magical land where unicorns fart rainbows and jokes would fall off trees.

Giggles.

Valerie: So did my credit card go through? Did you all get your drinks?

A man: Yes it did.

Valarie: Well shit. Hello financial chaos. At least it bought me a few moments of validity.

A man: Can we go back to you not knowing if you are real? I want you to prove it to me.

Valerie: That's not going to happen. Even I have my limits. Don't scar audience for life.

Giggles

Valerie: Tina Fey has this thing about her male co-workers pissing in jars. I was like, what's wrong with pissing in a jar? Eight people living in a one bathroom household has made this forty-two year old an expert.

Giggles.

Valerie: Like some competent person, I tweeted something to her along those lines. I didn't receive a response. I guess add delusional to my list of problems. Unicorn farts are gorgeous and they smell like lilacs.

Chuckles.

A woman: You have seven roommates and one bathroom? Damn you are Poor as fuck. Luckily I got a four dollar drink.

Valerie: No, my husband, our kids, his kids and a runaway.

A man: If you are married, why the fuck are you hitting on people? And asking of you can get laid? Does your husband not touch you?

Valerie: My, God, I wish. My husband won't keep his hands off me. I just need more than one person wanting me at a time or I am undesirable and ugly and stupid and fat and...

A woman: Shut up. Remember this is not pity comedy. I will beat your skinny ass if you say you are fat. I'd kill for my thigh to be as small as your waist. Shit.

Cheers

Valerie: Moving on, anyone like living in chaos?

A few claps.

Valerie: I have a love hate relationship with chaos. Sometimes chaos takes me out of the mundane and shows me a good time out on the town and it's true love.

Giggles.

Valerie: However, chaos will all of a sudden not agree with me and I puke everywhere.

Giggles.

Valerie: Looking at the vomit, I'm like oh there is a bad idea right there. Here's some sex I shouldn't have had over here. Wow, I wasted way too much money at the strip club. Did I really punch a chick?

Laughs.

Valerie: I feel like a lot of things disagree with me. Happiness for example, it comes in and wraps its warm blanket around me. Then happiness pours water on the blanket and I am sick and shivering. Fuck, I wish the good emotions would last longer.

A woman: Damn, Valerie, you really are a Debbie Downer.

Valerie: I'm sorry. I didn't stick to a script. I just wanted to be liked. I guess I should have figured. Nobody likes me. Hell, every goldfish I buy commits suicide by jumping out of its bowl. I'm like was it something I said?

Giggles.

A woman: Your husband sure seems to like you. And kids always love their mama.

Valerie: We went over this. One validation equals no validation. Imagine you got your parking garage ticket validated by the business you were just visiting and the parking attendant says it is not valid. So you start screaming at the attendant. This is me in a nutshell. One is never enough.

A Man: Do you want to fuck after the show as one person groping you is never enough?

Valerie: I'm not fucking anyone after the show, my husband included.

Man: I would validate you the whole time. You are definitely a unique individual.

Valerie: Thanks but no thanks. One thing I know about myself is that I would rather feel like a nobody than have sex with a stranger. I have certain limits believe it or not.

A woman: There you go, girl. You finally found something about yourself to respect.

Valerie: It's nothing to respect, it's such a minor thing that a lot of people do.

Woman: Jesus, Debbie! You made me laugh and you had the courage to come out here to perform. You must believe in yourself somewhat. Sorry people! I'll get off my soap box now.

Claps and a whistle.

Valerie: Girl, you must be joking. I came out here on a whim. It does not show self confidence or respect.

A man: You say tomato, we say ta-mat-o.

Valerie: Ok, whatever. I see the time is escaping from me now. The clock is like, oh shit, Valerie get your pathetic ass off the stage. I'll finish with one last joke. How many pathetic people does it take to screw in a light bulb? None, they just act helpless until someone does it for them.

Giggles

Valerie: Thanks for being a supportive audience. I will take what I can get. I'm broke but it was worth it. I can promise you that the next comic is going to make you want to piss your pants. He is fucking hilarious. Thanks again. I will be canceling my date with the razor blade and bathtub.

Giggles and applause.

Scene opens in a crowded DMV. There are three people waiting for their number to be called. One person is confidant Chrystal who is sitting. Another person is anxious Abby who is pacing. The third is self-loathing, self-sabotaging Sam who is also sitting all curled up on a chair. They are holding number 120. The sign is showing now serving 103.

Abby: (*pacing*) Oh my God. We are going to be waiting here the rest of our lives. This is inhumane. I swear the government wanted us to go crazy when the DMV was invented.

Chrystal: Stop being so dramatic. Yes there is a long wait time, but we will get out of here in a couple of hours.

Abby: I can't wait that long. It is too long. Just shoot me now.

Sam: (*looking up*) I would gladly shoot you if I could. It would ease the pounding headache I have.

Abby: I cannot help but worry so much that our head is pounding.

Sam: Yeah, no shit. I just think you should just accept that the worse is going to happen and we will be stuck in this purgatory that we call the DMV forever. And we wouldn't be in so much pain, my chest feels like it is caving in because of you.

Chrystal: I agree that the physical pain hurts but we need to be here and deal with it.

Abby: That is the fucking thing though. We don't NEED to be here. You just said we should be here because you wanted to have a better picture on our license.

Chrystal: Shut the fuck up. It is more than wanting to be looking better on the photo. Sure it is part of it. I mean come on our eyes look like they are crossed.

Sam: We might as well look that way. If we get pulled over when we are drinking our eyes will match the photo.

Abby: Ha, Ha, good one Sam. So why are we here then?

Chrystal: We have to renew the license anyway.

Abby: That could be done online. We are so old now we do not need an updated photo every renewal. So we are back to your goddamn vanity.

Chrystal: I am not vain.

Sam: You are so vain. You think you are good enough and then put yourself out there for others to judge.

Abby: Yeah. I am sick of being judged as well. I feel like all of these people here are talking about us behind our back. They are calling us basket cases.

Sam: Well you are a basket case. I swear you are putting a dent in the floor where you have been pacing for the last ten minutes.

Chrystal: I am sure they aren't talking about us. Look the number they are serving now is 105. We have killed time here by talking.

Abby: People are laughing. They are making fun of us. I hate you for dragging us out here. We are so vulnerable in the open.

Sam: I agree we could be home and making ourselves miserable without having other people make fun of us.

Chrystal: I am sure people are just joking amongst themselves to kill the time. I am sure they couldn't care less about us.

Sam: Unlike you who is insisting we wait in a long line to just to have a picture that looks nice. I don't fucking get you, Chrystal.

Chrystal: What do you mean?

Sam: You want us to look good on our license photo so other people will say oh that's a nice photo. You are phony as shit.

Abby: Yeah, Chrystal, you act so Goddamn confident yet you need other people to validate you.

Chrystal: What is wrong with needing to be validated? You two certainly do not help with our need for validation.

Sam: That's because I don't give a shit. I know that things always go wrong for us and I am realistic. You have your Goddamn head in the clouds. No one is going to validate us. Nor should they. We are a piece of shit. We always will be a piece of shit and frankly I am upset that you put us out there to be ridiculed.

Abby: Yeah, why do you do that to us? I like things just being status quo. I hate having new things to worry about.

Chrystal: We aren't talking about the license renewal anymore are we?

Abby: We were never talking about that. Sam and I are so pissed that you submitted the manuscript to a publisher.

Sam: I know. I told you the book was crap. I told you that we should just self-publish that piece of shit and waste all of our money and not sell a single fucking copy.

Chrystal: I don't know. I know the idea of the book has never been done before.

Sam: Just because it has never been done before doesn't mean that the writing is any good.

Abby: Yeah, you write me as if I am only a basket case. You do not show that I have positive qualities such as being able to help prepare for the future.

Sam: You didn't even give a shit about me. You did not include me in your writing as you just want to show that we are confident. You want to turn your back on me. I'm your own twin brother.

Chrystal: I am not turning my back on you. And yes, Abby, you do come across as just a shaken up bottle ready to explode at any second. However, that is all you have been giving me these last several months. You have yet to show me where you have made our future more comfortable given our circumstance.

Abby: That's because you fucking are pulling crap like sending in a manuscript for others to review and ridicule. I personally think that the idea is bullshit and like Sam says we need to self-publish or better yet, not publish at all.

Sam: Yeah, Chrystal, your fucking need for outside validation is bullshit. If you are so Goddamn confident, than why do you need someone to look at what you wrote and tell you it is good enough?

Chrystal: Come on that is not fair.

Abby: You are talking about fair? I fucking hate you. The number they are serving now is 110. We have already been here for hours.

Chrystal: We have not been here for hours.

Sam: We have been here a fucking long time considering we could have clicked a couple of buttons online and be renewed. I still think our picture would serve us well if we ever get pulled over while drinking.

Chrystal: You keep talking about drinking and driving. We are going the sober route again. I don't know why you are convinced that we will drink and drive.

Sam: You know how impulsive we can get. Especially when Abby is basically running in place as her nerves are too much to handle. It is a matter of a whim when driving to pull into a convenience store to get alcohol.

Abby: I know I feel like I am so close to doing that right now. Like fuck waiting for our number to come up. We should leave here, get alcohol and drink while we renew online. That way the people here will stop making fun of us. Chrystal, it is a sick way to be validated.

Chrystal: I am not looking to be validated by the people here waiting at the DMV. They are in the same boat of having to wait for forever and again I am sure they are not talking about us. Abby, with your pacing I am sure they have noticed us so our existence is validated.

Abby: I wouldn't be pacing so much if we just did things the safe way.

Sam: Yeah, your confidence is supposed to be a good thing but because we are who we are, I always have a great impact on you.

Chrystal: Yes I know. Both of you have a great impact on me. I still think that getting an outside opinion on the book is better than just relying on our own opinion.

Sam: Yeah, because my opinion is that the book is shit. No one will read it. The writing is poor. We look like we do not have a grasp on the English language. The book is unique as it has never been done before. Did you ever once stop to think that it has never been done before for a reason. The reason being that it is an asinine idea.

Chrystal: Well you do rub off on me twin brother. I have thought that. I just need to have a professional tell me that the book is bad. Then I will know to give up on this book and write another. It only took us around 100 days to write it.

Abby: Well, shit. What are we supposed to do if the one person who thinks we have any sort of talent and has any confidence what so ever is doubting the book.

Chrystal: I am not doubting the book. I am a tiny bit worried that the book would not be sellable. I know my goal was to have a book that could help people. Even if no one writes any of their own psychoscribble, I think it is still good in that it really explains what is going on in the mind of someone with BPD.

Sam: If you are worried that the book might not be sellable, than why send it to a publisher?

Chrystal: Well, we need the outside validation. We need to know that a publisher thinks that the book is printable. The company I sent the manuscript to specialists in new authors. That is us, new author, as we gave up our passion for writing to work at an awful job and spend the rest of the time floating in alcohol. I wish I didn't need the outside validation myself. We might very well get a thank you for manuscript, however we do not believe it is publishable. At least we would know that we would have to totally revamp the book before self publishing.

Sam: Chrystal, we think you should just bypass everything. You should realize that we are not talented and just self publish. You are giving Abby a heart attack. I cannot believe the pain we are in right now just because you need to be validated.

Abby: He is not joking. You are killing me, Chrystal. We still have a wait for our number to be called as at 116 now. It is this waiting that is killing me. How long did they say to hear back on the book?

Chrystal: They said two to three weeks.

Abby: Are you shitting me? That is longer than this line at the DMV.

Chrystal: I know, I am sorry. I just wish the two of you would see why I needed to do this. I needed to put myself out there. I need to be vulnerable. I just need that little extra boost to validate the writing.

Sam: We are probably not going to get that boost.

Abby: I know I am going nuts.

Chrystal: Well, if we get a rejection we just need to work harder.

Sam: We could just give up just as easily. We could just be on disability and not do anything productive with our lives.

Chrystal: I do not want that and I know you guys don't want that either in your heart of hearts. You want us to have something to live for. I think getting our book out there and donating a lot of copies would at least be something. We did not write the book to make money. We wrote the book for our own healing as psychoscribble is my favorite form of psychotherapy.

Sam: So why not leave it at that? Why try and get the book published?

Chrystal: We need to create a life worth living. Writing is going to be a part of that. I think advocating for mental health awareness is another part of the life worth living. I am confident that the book will help at least one person out there. It would just be a matter of reaching that one person. I will self publish if it comes down to it.

Abby: The whole thing is nerve wracking. I am not at all happy. I just want to get out of here. I need to know what is going on with the book so I could notify Dexter that he maybe should step up to the plate. Maybe Anita would need to be involved.

Chrystal: You are just assuming the worse. I feel like we need to just be patient and sit back and wait. I am hoping I will receive my much needed validation. If I don't, than I just know I need to work harder.

Sam: I still think this whole thing is bullshit as even with your confidence you still need others to tell you that you are good.

Chrystal: You know we need that as we cannot do it for ourselves. Well, I can validate myself a bit, however it is not enough. It is never enough.

Abby: Oh my God. We just got an email from the publisher. That was fast it was supposed to be up to three weeks and here it is only one week. That's probably a bad sign.

Chrystal: I know our number will be up in a second here. I kinda want to look at what it says before we get our picture taken.

Sam: Yes, you should do that. Won't it be so funny when we take the picture and it's even worse as you are going to get bad news. You realize that, Chrystal. We are hearing back too soon so it's going to be bad news.

Abby: I can't even tell you what to do here. I want to know so I can stop worrying about it. I also would rather not know in case if it is going to crush us.

Chrystal: It is not going to crush us. I just need to look at it. (*looks at phone*). Holy shit. They want to give our book a chance.

Abby: I feel like I can breathe again.

Sam: Wow, imagine that. Make sure it's not a scam.

Chrystal: It is not a scam. It is a company that specializes in new authors. We pay a small fee but we will get the book edited. This is great. Oh, our number is up. We can finally take the picture and we should look a lot more relaxed since last time.

They walk up to the counter. End scene.

CHAPTER TEN

The Endless Pit

The feeling of emptiness is fairly hard to describe; my psycho-scribble to follow is the closest I can get. It is a feeling that seems to be very specific to those who have BPD. It almost feels like a part of me. The feeling is constant. I have gone through periods of time I do not feel this. Boredom only exasperates the feeling of empty.

Boredom is very hard for me to tolerate. I know it is not just myself who feels this way. It is recommended that people with BPD work or volunteer for at least twenty hours a week. We need the structure, for one thing. I think the main reason though is to stave off the boredom. People with BPD really need to be kept busy to get away from the empty pit. We need to feel valued.

I know that my empty pain has led me to picking unhealthy quick fixes as of late. Drinking and overeating sweets is not healthy for me. I feel like I need it as the open cave echoes the need to be filled. When I am bored, I have nothing to fill this void. I find myself to be highly suicidal when I am bored and empty. The hospital thought that my depression and suicidal ideation was strictly based on my situation. I changed my situation by getting out of my job and here I am still highly suicidal. I think the hospital underestimated how sick I actually am. I present well. I am the depressed person who gets out of bed and forces herself to exercise and shower everyday. I cannot do housework or socialize, but I present as though I am not depressed. My BPD was underestimated. The empty pain along with boredom is the true reason I feel suicidal. I enjoy writing this book through my recovery, but it is not structured enough for me. It doesn't make me feel like I am important. Once this book touches one person's life is when I will feel the purpose and will market the book to the best of my ability. I hope that will be enough to keep my mind busy.

With boredom, I only have my racing thoughts to deal with. I try and do things to keep busy such as reading, writing, artwork, video games, and watching TV. However, when I am feeling extremely bored and empty, these distractions are not enough. I am back to researching ways to die online. This has staved off the boredom and emptiness. I know it is not healthy though. My other distractions are healthy. After my reading on suicide makes me feel better, I go to one of my coping skills and it is easier. I have to go to one of my coping skills or my obsession will lead me to a suicidal gesture. I wish the coping skills would always work the first time and I didn't have to use an unhealthy method to feel better. I know there is nothing wrong with suicidal ideation. I am just looking for peace. As long as I can use it to just get over my hump of empty boredom, it isn't the worst thing I could do.

The following piece of writing is a prose to best describe the feeling to those who do not understand what it means to feel empty. I hope there are others who can relate to this. This piece is basically a flow of conscious piece based on my feeling of emptiness. This is not a bad way to journal. As long as you have the thought or feeling you want to explore and then you just stick with it, it's a tamed monkey to mind. I think having a plan of what to write about before you actually sit down is the key to successful journaling.

The Cave

I am awoken. The air is very still. Hard to breathe. Laying on hard ground, I push myself up. Ouch. A stalactite runs into my brain. I am in a dream. Deja vu. Not a dream. Real, real life. What is life? Is it this cave? I slowly walk winding around the stalagmites and avoiding the stalactites the best I can. It is dark. I cannot breathe. Why must I be here again? There is no easy way out. I walk further and further into the abyss. Darkness surrounds me. I cannot breathe. Get me out of here. I trip and bump my head endless times. It feels like an eternity has gone by. Pain and darkness. I do not remember if I ever escaped here before? Did I? I cannot remember. I can only remember each step I take. Every bruise and scar I gain are familiar. I think I am home. Is this really where I live? It must be. It's so dark and familiar. I don't remember the way out. The more I walk I feel myself descending deeper and deeper. I don't want to keep going. I am pulled. Imaginary rope around my waist. I cannot breathe. My chest aches. I need to get out of this pit. The further I walk the stalagmites and stalactites get fewer and far between. The new yet familiar dark is empty. It's heavy. I cannot see. There is no way out. I remember was there a time I left this cave? I must have. I thought it was a dream. I must know life outside of the darkness. I cannot remember it though. Maybe it doesn't exist. What is real? Empty, hollow, shallow breaths. This is home. Why isn't there a door? I cannot remember. The feeling brings me back to childhood when I would run to my imagination to escape. Can I do that now? I try and the images wont come. I need to sleep. Sleep is when I can breathe. I need help. No one around. Echoes of my childhood start ringing in my ears. I have been here for a long time. I am just now hearing my voice from ages ago. I guess I have never found my way out? I can only feel the heavy, hollow pain in my chest. An earthquake has gone through me. I am stuck falling. Falling and falling. The canyon never ends. It must end. Back to what I perceive is reality. I have footing on the dark cave floor. Walking, arms out stretched. Nothing ahead of me. Nothing behind. Just the empty, painful darkness.

CHAPTER ELEVEN

I Feel You

Fairly recent research has found that many people with Borderline Personality Disorder are empaths. I am one of the many. From reading a few articles on the internet, I think the opposite was believed in the past and from what I have gathered it was because of our emotion regulation issues. I have always been told that I am too sensitive as I was growing up. I think my empathy has something to do with it. My mother has felt like she has had to walk on eggshells around me. I believe that this is true as I am highly sensitive to others emotions, especially if the emotions are "negative." When my mother feels sad, I cannot help but feel sad myself.

The first time I remember feeling what others felt was when I was a child. I was between the ages of five to seven. I do not remember exactly how old I was, but I can still bring up the feeling that I had back then. I was brought to a funeral for my mother's friend's grandmother. I met this woman only a few times. I had no feelings towards her. However, at the funeral I felt this heaviness in my chest. I kept sighing. I felt like crying but knew there was no reason for me to cry as I was not close to the deceased. I couldn't figure out why I felt so heavy and yet empty at the same time. I did not tell anyone about my feelings as I thought that they were stupid feelings to have. I cannot believe that I can still remember what I felt back then still to this day. Empathy of taking on the sadness of others had great impact on me. I did not know that what I was feeling was that of empathy. I just thought that I had odd feelings that I could not figure out.

I also get very sad when I hear about tragedy on the news. I sometimes cannot eat when the news is super painful. The useless, endless deaths from mass shootings affect me deeply. I feel a pit in my stomach and I have a hard time swallowing the food I am consuming at the time, so I end up needing to throw it out. I eventually gave up watching the news altogether. I like being informed as to what is going on in the world. However, I prefer to not feel the pain the news causes me. I have to quickly scroll past anything political or news based on social media. I know a lot of people have a hard time watching the news. A few of these people told me they need to turn off the news when they hear about senseless deaths. I don't know if they feel the same stabbing pain as I do. They mostly explain that their anger gets to them. Of course, all of the people I have had a conversation about the news with have been people with mental health issues. There definitely is a link of those who struggle with mental illness and that of empathy. We feel deeply and can relate to others pain.

I can gauge when people are sad or angry very easily. I do pick up on the positive emotions of others. Unfortunately the happiness of others doesn't do too much to lift my depressed mood. I know it does help. It just doesn't resonate with me as much as sadness does. When someone I am very close to feels sad, I am highly affected by this. I get the same deep, heavy, empty pain I got when I was a child. I try to not let it affect me, but it always does. I am feeling this great sadness so deeply that it becomes my own. I feel like I am to blame for the loved one's sadness, and I just feel worse about myself. I will sometimes turn this sadness into an argument. I often go from feeling anger that turns to sadness or vice versa. I end up inadvertently lashing out. I do not want to do this as the loved one is probably feeling worse than I am as the pain originated with them. I hate when my emotions take over and that is one of the biggest issues that I am working on as I write this book.

When I worked at the phone company, my empathy was a gift and a curse at the same time. When customers grew angry, I felt the anger entering my ears, and, like a waterfall, it washed over my entire body. When the customer was angry because of a problem that we created, I would feel anger right along with them. I was enraged at the company I was working for because they decided it was fine to miss someone's install day after day. I agreed one hundred percent with these customers. I would stuff down my rage towards the company. I would be polite and apologetic to the customer. I would be cursing at myself on the inside as I decided to work at a job where I had to bend the truth constantly. I would curse management at the same time, but I would have to take out the anger on myself.

If I had a customer who was angry and calling me names because they did something wrong such as not paying their bill, I would lash back. I would not yell at the customer or anything along those lines. I would end up getting very condescending and would turn the words they said to me to stab them right back. This was when my empathy was a curse. I always wanted to treat every customer fairly and equally. This was often not the case. I blame my empathy and my intense feelings. I would be upset with myself for being rude to a customer. I just lose sight of my filter sometimes. Again, I would never yell and I never swore at a customer. I would bottle as much of the anger as I could. The result of this was me getting home and exploding.

I would drink and dull out the anger. I often got so carried away about complaining about a customer that Jason would say that I should calm down and take it down a notch. He said this before I told him I have BPD. Therefore, he did not understand that I couldn't help my escalated anger. I had not had any treatment specifically for my BPD until I was 42. Jason would then get an angry earful from me in which I said he didn't care about my feelings and I would then continue to fight or go isolate.

I like being empathetic as I can really listen to others. If a friend of mine is sad and going through a rough time, I love to talk to her. I know I feel the pain a bit as they talk about their heartbreak or suffering. However, it is because of my empathy that I provide a good sounding board. I do love to help others whenever I can. It is in my nature to do so. I would love to be a peer support staff at some point in time. I believe that my general sense of understanding and kindness would be a great attribute in helping others. Heck, I am writing this book with the goal to help others who are struggling like I am or to help those in the field to truly understand what goes on in the brain of a person with BPD.

CHAPTER TWELVE

The End? No, just a new beginning

The writing of my book has given me a reason to keep on keeping on. I am sure that it has saved my life. I had the book and reached out for help every time I was heading to a hotel. It is now January 2019 and things are still up in the air. I feel like I have been getting better over these past four weeks. Granted, I have been going from one facility to the other since December 3rd. I am at a different outpatient facility at this time. I am picking up new things in this dual diagnosis partial hospital program. I am past 30 days sober again and feel the strength I had when I was nine months sober. I foresee that sobriety will continue in my journey.

I am at a crisis stabilization unit as I type these words on January 6th, 2019. I have three more days here, and if I didn't have my laptop, you would not want to see the crazy mess I would be. Writing has been my savior. I also am holding onto that hope that at least one person will gain insight from my words and experiences. I know that I have mentioned my love-hate relationship with hope. Today I love hope.

I mostly wrote this book for myself. I am driven, however, that someone will pick up the book and say, "Oh, my, God. This is my life. There is someone out there just like me. She has stumbled and fallen several times, but she has found a glimmer of hope. Perhaps I can find the one thing that will drive me to stay alive." This has been my goal for the book. I needed it to help me on my own recovery path. The hope comes in with the thought it could help people. Even if no one takes any of my writing ideas to their journals, it is still a success as long as people can gain understanding of the borderline mind. I definitely can see this book helping out therapists as well. My raw writing shows the struggle borderlines go through on a daily basis. Perhaps a therapist will take the journaling ideas and suggest one or two to their patients.

I am so thankful that I have Dr. Price as my psychiatrist. I do not think I would have had the courage to write a book without him. He sparked my love of writing very early on in our professional relationship. I had to write a brief biography so he could have my background in order to work with me better. My brief autobiography ended up being sixteen pages. I had forgotten that I loved to write nonfiction as much as I liked writing poems, which I got back into when I was in rehab.

2018 was a year of learning. I still do not know exactly who I am. I guess it doesn't really matter. The times I don't feel like I am real is a bit more difficult. I am sure with my continuation of treatment I will find a way to feel whole most of the time. Here in 2019, I am going to have a completely new model for recovery. I will have a team, a social worker, a case worker, and a med manager. I will not be able to see my current providers during this time. It sucks, but it is for the best. They say this is the second best treatment to hospitalization and partial hospital. I hope this is true. I want to say I am cautiously optimistic, but I fear (darn that anxiety) that it won't work to make me completely better. There will be a few groups I will attend. My meds are going to be on lockdown, and I need to pick them up daily. I will have the ability to reach out to someone on the team 24/7. This is helpful. I just fear that because the treatment is based on DBT, I won't get enough out of it. I have gained some insights through DBT. For me I have to write about the lessons that are taught or I do not get to wise mind. We will just have to see what will happen though. Perhaps I will be doing enough writing that I could write a sequel to this book, "My continuation of treatment to full recovery." That is always a possibility. It does depend on the popularity of this book of course. If this book doesn't break me even for the amount I paid for editing, I probably will write the sequel just for myself. I do have the lowest list price on the book as it is not about the money for me. I paid extra to take off $4.00 from the original list price. The book is about helping myself and as many other people as I can.

I am not sure if full recovery for me is feasible. With the right treatment, many people with BPD do recover fully. I want to be one of them. If I cannot recover fully, I at least want to get to a spot where I can control my symptoms. Who knows, maybe that is considered full recovery for those with BPD. I guess it might be semantics. I am feeling better now. I have not felt suicidal in over four days now. This is huge for me as it was a very consistent thought for most of 2018.

I do not know at this time as to what is going to happen with my marriage. I do not know when I will be allowed to move back home. I might never be able to move back in. I am trying to accept this reality. It is hard for me to do so. I need to control what I can and that is keeping myself safe and not having another affair. Amy has a girlfriend now, so at least that affair piece has been cut off super easily. I just need to validate myself and learn to accept Jason's validation.

I have begun writing in a journal specifically designated to gratitude. Studies show that having gratitude has a positive effect on health and overall wellness. I know I have many things to be grateful for, but I usually don't think about them. I have been trying to write down three things I am grateful for in the morning and three things at night. I wouldn't doubt if this has something to do with my reduction in suicidal ideation. I would recommend for everyone to at least think about three things you are grateful for each day. Even if it is like a placebo, it really does help.

I am fearful about my future. I am going to continue to write. I am going to continue to work towards a life worth living. Goodbye for now, maybe you will see more writing from me. Perhaps you will see a piece of fictional writing. Thank you for reading. I hope you got at least one thing out of my book.

The author

Kirsten Shonle is a first-time author from Portland, ME where she lives with her husband and three boys. Shonle is introverted, artistic, creative, and humorous. Outside of writing, she also enjoys painting, reading, and creating memes. When she was fourteen, Shonle moved with her family from Colorado to Maine. Her husband supports her and her mental illness, and she loves her three humorous boys and two stepchildren. Shonle's mission is to become an advocate to end the stigma that surrounds mental illness.

novum 📖 PUBLISHER FOR NEW AUTHORS

The publisher

He who stops getting better stops being good.

This is the motto of novum publishing, and our focus is on finding new manuscripts, publishing them and offering long-term support to the authors.
Our publishing house was founded in 1997, and since then it has become THE expert for new authors and has won numerous awards.

Our editorial team will peruse each manuscript within a few weeks free of charge and without obligation.

You will find more information about novum publishing and our books on the internet:

www.novumpublishing.com

www.ingramcontent.com/pod-product-compliance
Lightning Source LLC
Chambersburg PA
CBHW021223090426
42740CB00006B/356